# A Girl Wizard

An autobiography by

Victoria Maclean

# Acknowledgements

I'd like to thank so many people for helping me through some really tough times. My amazing husband Adam. Monica, Daniel, Harry, Jess, Hannah and Matt.

To Mel my friend from school who was one of the only people to understand how hard it was losing my mum even though so many of my friends really tried.

My sister Dee and my brother Lawrence, even though they both drive me crazy. My amazing in-laws who have shown me how family should be treated. I love you all.

All the Maclean's and Phillips on my husband's side of the family.

My Uncle Paul who should have been my dad. I will always love you. All the Whiting's even though I haven't seen them for years.

My Uncle Nic who is off his head but so funny.

My wonderful Harry Potter Collector UK and Fantastic Beasts UK page Editors Beverly, Janice and Charlotte.

To Collin and Sam for all the amazing items and for being there for me. I love you both so much.
To Luca from Retro Styler on line for all my incredible freebies.

To MinaLima for helping me see what beauty is in so many ways.

My incredible Harry Potter friends, Sean Valentine, Kelly White, and Johnnie Blue. I think your utterly crazy.

Anthony and Justine for putting up with me all these years.

To JK Rowling, with whom I think a lot of us would be in very different circumstances if it wasn't for her incredible Wizarding World that helped us to escape and all become the amazing people we are today.

All my friends and fans on social media. I could not of got as far as I have today without your love and support. You are the best friends and  fans ever!

So sorry if I have forgotten anyone. I'm sure I will be reminded very soon.

Oh and Gemma, Nic and Laura for taking Harry to school when I was called in early on set and all the other school Mums for putting up with my endless posts. Your all amazing. I couldn't have got here without you.

And most especially my Mum for some of the best memories I could ever have asked for. She was a Harry Potter superfan and my hero. I miss you mum. I love you, always xxxx

# Special Note

Here is a special message from Victoria's sister.

"I would just like to say something to those people who feel the need to judge her on what she has been through. She felt the need to write a book about how she has got to where she is today. From a very young age she has seen and dealt with more than any child should have to deal with. I tried my best as her big sister to protect her and our brother from the saddest times in our lives. Not always successful i know but I too was only young. Thankfully my sister was spared from seeing and hearing a lot and for that I am grateful.

I honestly didn't think she would become as successful as she has and I am incredibly proud of her. Yes, I read her book and yes it was so damn hard and in places I hurt but I completely understand why she wrote it. She could have walked down a very dark path, any of us could of but we didn't and that was because it didn't matter how ill our mum was she did the best job she could to make sure we were loved. Our mum was incredible! Our Father didn't and he made our lives, all of us including our mum, hell! We lived in fear constantly.

So, for those people who have objected to what Victoria has written need to back off! She wrote the truth and she needed to do it. No one who hurts someone that much should be protected. Those who have been badly hurt and made it through to the other side need to be celebrated.

Victoria, you have come a million miles and now look at you.....You're an inspiration to so many, including me. I love you"

xxxxxxxxxx "always" ☐ xxxxxxxxxxx

Since publishing my story, I have endured endless trolling from some of my father's family. It has been horrific and terrifying. Something I wouldn't wish on any one. His family just don't want the world to know the truth and hate that I am  telling my horrific story. I'm sorry, but you cannot keep me quite anymore!

Victoria

# I Love Magic

It's amazing when you consider where I started, to where I have ended up. I'm not writing this story for people to feel sorry for me. I'm sure there are many people who have been through similar or worse than I have. This is to show my readers, what you can do with your life if you try, no matter what has happened to you in the past. I want people to think, oh my God, this girl has gone from this to this. Well hats off to her.

I was born in the Royal Berkshire hospital, near Reading back in 1980 to Sue and Peter. I was the youngest of three. My Sister Nadean is seven years older and my brother Lawrence is five years older than me. My dad had left the Army and was now working as a window fitter while my mum ran the local playgroup in our village. When I was seven we moved to West Wales, after the company my dad was working for went bankrupt. Why they decided to move to rural West Wales I don't know. But to this day I still call Wales my home.

"Every time I see you, you're walking. We call you 'The Walker' because we don't know your real name." I stood there and laughed. During my younger years I would walk for miles and miles. It was the best way to leave my troubles behind and just breath in the fresh, clean air of South West Wales. I was chatting to a local man from the village I was living in at the time, Clynderwen near Haverfordwest, because my mum and dad had separated.

Six Months before, my dad had attacked my brother Lawrence in our house. This was nothing new, but this time, my mum saw it with her own eyes, so she threw my dad out. I, being only 14 at the time, didn't know anything about it until I went downstairs to see my dad and he wasn't there. When we were younger, my dad took his aggression out on us. It was always so frightening, he was a "control freak" and would become angry and shout at us, for simple things like looking in the fridge for a snack. We nicknamed him "God" which he hated. But this was all that we knew. To be fair though, my sister got it worse than my brother and me, but my sister managed to move out to become a stable groom at the age of fifteen. My dad would really only do things when mum was out. He would then tell her that we fell over or hit our heads. She would never have believed us if we had told her the truth. I remember a time when I was about eight, I wet the bed. I had a weak bladder so this wasn't unusual. My dad came upstairs to my room and pulled me over his knees and just kept hitting me. My sister screamed at him to stop but he just kept going. I don't remember what happened after that but this was just a small example of his anger. I remember another time when my mum was out and it was just me and my dad in the house again. I remember I was still wearing my school uniform. I can't recall what he was angry at, but I do have memories of running for the back door, but as I got the door open he stopped me. I somehow managed to get half way out of the door and he slammed the door against my head banging my head against the door frame and the door. He told mum I fell. It wasn't until mum say his anger with her own eyes that she started to see his true side.

After mum kicked my dad out of the house, we moved to Clynderwen and my dad moved back in to the family home. Clynderwen was only a small village but the house we moved to was nice enough. It was called Glendale Villa. I finally lived near children my own age and had a park to play in. Yes, I was in my teens but I was very young for my age to start with. I just wanted to play all the time. Living there didn't stop me from walking though. Running through Clynderwen was a train track. Whenever it was nice, I would walk along a small walk way that ran parallel to the train tracks. It was a stunning walk and I loved seeing the trains passing me.

Being in this village made me grow up fast though. I was noticing boys, I had friends who were a little older than me but I wasn't a bad child. OK, maybe that's a little lie. I did go skinny dipping with a friend from school, Glen Goodman at Pendine beach and then told mum that I had missed the train back home and went out in Carmarthen instead but I didn't get drunk. I was fifteen so I was still too young in my eyes. See, I wasn't all bad until not long after.

After eighteen months of separation my dad managed to convince mum that he had changed and they finally got back together. So, myself and mum moved back into the family home. During the eighteen months, my brother had moved away to live with his girlfriend in London so it was just me left. To be fair, from what I remember, dad had calmed down. Until one day during an argument, he went right up to my face and dared me to hit him. Something inside me snapped and I kept punching him in the stomach over and over again. He didn't move, all 6 foot 2 and 17 stone of him. I managed to run past him screaming as I ran up the stairs. I got to my room and slammed the door. I sat on my bed and cried. After about five minutes, he entered. He sat down next to me on my bed and said that I really hurt his tummy. I think that's when he realised how much he scared and hurt me. After that day, his temper seemed to calm down, to a point.

My mum was a fantastic mum, always telling us she loved us and asked for hugs but also to clean up after ourselves and to say please and thank you. To always be polite to others no matter what and if I started to pick up a Welsh twang from school, she would correct me, after all, she was bought up in Kensington. My mum was an incredibly creative woman too. When I was younger, I was always amazed at what she was capable of. mum would make pictures out of saw dust. The kind you would find in saw mills or used to line rabbit hutches. She would put some of them on to a baking tray and cook them in the oven till they were the exact colour she wanted. She would do this several times till she had all different shades and then set to work making pictures.

My dad would sand a piece of thick wood, about three inches thick, in to a certain shape like a wooden canvas. mum would have a picture in mind next to the wood and set to work. She would have all the different shades of saw dust on a tray like a painting pallet and carefully stick them on one at a time. Like a mosaic until there was an amazing mosaic of *The Mary Rose* or

*The Flying Scotsman* train in front of you. She would then varnish over the entire thing and there you would have an incredible picture all made of wood carvings. To this day I have never found anything like it and I couldn't tell you where they all were now. I do remember that our old neighbours had 1 in their front room or use to. mum would do these as gifts for friends or sell them at car boot sales. She just loved doing them.

Another of her talents was drawing. In fact, there was a hand draw pictures my mum drew of a king fisher bird hanging up in the doctor's surgery where she resided until recently. It had been hanging there since I was very young. mum also had an incredible talent with coloured wax. She had a special iron with no holes on the flat part. She would melt a certain colour wax onto the iron and then iron a piece of photo card. mum did this with all different colours and then use tools like a soldering iron or a needle to make finer detail or scratch details into the picture. She would do blue bells, daffodils, daisies, castles, fields, rivers, streams, all sorts of pictures. There was nothing she couldn't do with her talent. She was a remarkable woman. mum was also an incredible pianist and guitar player. I remember hearing her play the piano on the weekends or weekday evenings. She was so talented. My sister and I would sing with her as she would play. We would sing songs from The Sound of Music or Memories, the Broadway musical. These were the happy memories I have and I truly value them.

I like to think that determination comes from my incredible mother. As she didn't finish school, mum went back to do her A levels when I was fifteen and passed them with high scores. mum went back and did theatre. She loved anything to do with acting, or performing, but I think music and art was her number one passion. Like me, I feel she found escape in it. A way to be creative and be at peace with the world but this isn't what she wanted to be when she was younger. My mum joined the army when I think she was around 16 or 17 and became an ambulance driver. She loved driving fast which I think I inherited too. Later on, when I was around nine, mum became a jalopy driver. In the words of Google, a jalopy driver is someone who drives a terrible car in the land of psychopaths. This makes me laugh because yes it was crazy, but mum was really good. It's funny because her email address was psychosue LOL. She became the Jalopy woman's champion for West Wales in 1989 and took home the biggest trophy I had ever seen which sat on top of the piano for a year until it had to be returned. Over the years mum has tried all sorts of things to escape but behind closed doors she had a lot of problems.

From a very young age, my mum has suffered with depression, anxiety and mental health. Even though mum always poorly, she would try to spoil us rotten for Christmas and birthdays. We never wanted for anything toy wise. When I was little, I wanted to be a nurse so I could help mum get better. When I was told she had to go away for work, she was really going into hospital for treatment but when she was at home, I remember she went back to bed a lot. I was told she wasn't feeling well. I hated this because this was when my dad's true side would come out. So, I would either stay in my room or go out for a walk. Trying to recall my past is quite painful but for the sake of closer I will try. I remember even in the warm sun, mum would wear long sleeve tops. At first, I just didn't think anything of it but later on as I got older, I started to see why and it hurts me to this day. My mum had a terrible problem with self-harming.

Now before you start judging her (the woman who was my very own Lilly Potter) she was given up by her own Mother when she was five. Before this she was sexually abused by her uncle and didn't know what she was doing from one day to the next. Her mother chose her boyfriend over her own children, my mum and two younger brothers. He didn't like children or want them. Luckily my mum was adopted by a couple who wanted children of their own, but sadly it would be a little longer for her two younger brothers, Nicolas and Paul, to find a home. My Uncle Paul and my Uncle Nic were adopted by Lord and Lady Haywood, who worked for Prince Charles and Lady Diana. Uncle Nic, is Nicolas Haywood the Spokesperson for the infamous Priory of Sion and a 33rd degree Freemason. We had been out of touch for several years, but I managed to track him down again and we have become very close. My Uncle Paul tragically died on a beach in Morocco before I had a chance to meet him.

When I was eleven, my mum met my brother and I at the bus stop after school one day after school. She said to Lawrence, "I'll give you £100 if you can tell me what news I heard today?" for that amount of money, my brother just said anything, but my mum knew that her money would be safe. She then told us that she had found out she had a brother. mum had contacted a company to try and find her real mum. It was expensive but she needed the closure it would bring. Months later they told her that her mum had passed away, and that she had, in fact, two younger brothers. mum was then told that the younger of the two had died years before but that the older brother Nic, was alive and well and wanted to meet her too. They got in contact a few days later and two weeks later Uncle Nic was on his way down for a visit from Derby where he resided. It was both exciting and terrifying. When we met him, it was amazing to see just how much Uncle Nic and my mum looked alike. Nic was so funny. He did all these impressions and had us laughing so hard. He told lots of jokes but at the age of eleven, I had no idea what they were about but as you do, you laugh anyway. Nic was also a member of the magic circle and told us about a £1 coin he used to have that you could put a pen or pencil through. Apparently, it was so realistic that he accidentally spent it one day and when he went back to the shop after realising his mistake, he had the cashier trying to shove pencils through all the pound coins to try and find which one it was. They eventually did. Then sadly a few days later he had to return home.

My mother's adopted father Frank, was the most incredible caring, wonderful and thoughtful man you could ever meet. He was a sweetheart and was totally devoted to his new adopted daughter. His wife, not so much. She loved my mother, don't get me wrong, but she was so hard on her and in her eyes my mum couldn't do a thing right. When I was three, her adopted mum became very ill. When my mum when to see her, she blamed my mum for giving her a cold. She died a few days later and mum never forgave herself after that. mum soon became worse, she was taking all sorts of medication and to a point it worked. I'm not too sure what happened over the next few years because, being the youngest, a lot was hidden from me by my older siblings. My sister, who always swore she didn't like me, was very protective and so was my older brother. I would hide in my room a lot of the time and live in my fantasy world where I would play a princess locked in a tall tower awaiting the day my prince would rescue me. Being surrounded by magic, unicorns and fairies in pictures all over my bedroom walls. That was where my dreams would take me when I needed to hide, until my father wanted to punish me for something. Then my bedroom door couldn't hide me for long.

I think the truth of my mother's illness finally hit me the time I was told by my father to watch her. I didn't know why, but I needed to watch her so he could go to the shop and get some milk. About 10 minutes later, my mum told me she needed some air, having put on her denim jacket, it looked like she was hiding something as she walked out of the house. Being my mum, I couldn't tell her what to do, plus I was only fifteen at the time. About 20 minutes later she came back in to the house saying that Pete (my father) was going to be extremely angry. When I looked down her arm and hand were covered in blood. She had taken a piece of glass and cut herself so deep that she needed an operation to repair the damage. I just kept repeating to her that it would be OK but the truth was I had no idea what to do. I was shaking. This was such a shock that I don't remember anything after that.

As you can imagine, I have blocked a lot of my childhood out over the years. My school years are almost a total blur. I can't remember most of the people I went to school with unless they played a big part in either being a friend or bullying me. My old friend Grace would regularly joke and ask me whether I actually went to school because there is so much and so many people I just can't remember. Writing this autobiography is bringing some of it back but only some. I'm sure there are many reasons for this and to be honest, I'm quite thankful.

When I was young all I wanted to do was shut the world out and live in my fantasies. A world where no one dies or hurts you. It's a scary world out there and one I needed to escape whenever I could, so I became fantasy mad. With audio books about Princes and Princesses, Queens and evil queens, good vs evil, long golden hair, magic flowers, witches and wizards. So, for me Harry Potter was simply perfect. My only wish is that it could have been released years earlier, so I could have escaped sooner.

I do remember when I would come home from school. I would turn on BBC 1 and get ready to watch Blue Peter. I loved that programme and continued to watch it even into my late teens. I couldn't tell you what year it was. I don't even remember them mentioning "Harry Potter" by name. But I do remember them talking about magic and a story about a Boy Wizard. This was my introduction to JK Rowling's Wizarding World. Anything about magic has always peeked my imagination. Anything for me to escape, no matter how fantastical it was. I wanted so badly for magic to exist, so I could change my life. Harry Potter seemed a long way from home to me so it was the perfect escape. Later in my life it would leave me with so much to be thankful for.

JK Rowling, we truly love you and thank you for giving us the world of Harry Potter.

# The Class Clown

Now my mum was an incredible lady and totally devoted to her children but there was one thing she couldn't stop – and that was me being bullied at school. I have forgotten a lot of my past but writing this is bringing some of it back. I do have one thing to be thankful for though, if we had social media back then it could have been a lot worse.

When I was in school I really struggled with learning. I couldn't read or write and I couldn't even write my own last name, so when we moved to Wales at the age of seven, being put in a Welsh school, was probably the worst thing that could have happened to me, or so I thought.

My first Welsh school was Beca Primary school in South West Wales. It was a small school with small classroom sizes. At first, I was the popular kid because I was pretty and new, then after a short time, my lack of reading and writing skills became apparent, but instead of being helped and tested for learning disabilities, the Head Master, Mr. Phillips, decided that making fun of me was more effective. After I would complete my work, he would make me and only me stand at the front of the class room while he read out my work. So, the whole class would laugh at me. He was a horrible teacher and one person I'm sorry to say I wouldn't spit on him if he was on fire. I went to that school for two years so not only was my home life horrible but my school life was as well.

Finally, my time there came to an end and I started secondary school. Ysgol Gyfun Dyffren Taf comprehensive school in Whitland. This is the same school that Mike Phillips attended, the famous scrum half for Wales. In fact, he was a few years below me and so short back then. He was so cute and covered in freckles. Mike had stunning blue eyes and was a little bugger but we called him Mikey.

As soon as I started Whitland, Mr. Thomas, the head of class room support realised I had disabilities straight away and I had help from day one. When I joined Whitland, I apparently had the reading age of a six-year-old at the age of eleven. They did an incredible job helping me though and for this I will love Mr. Thomas forever. Unfortunately, this didn't change things for me being bullied. I was picked on throughout my entire school life. I'm still not sure to this day why but I think it's because I was different. I didn't want to follow trends, I didn't want to sleep around, or smoke or do drugs, so because I had my own ideas and learning difficulties I was bullied.

From what I remember of school, it wasn't all bad. I had a few friends but only a few, I passed my GCSEs and I went to college. My home life was still the same. Horrible and isolated. I would go for really long walks when things got bad, because as I grew older I realised being out of the house was far better for me then being inside and an easy target for my father's aggression.

I made friends with two young girls in the village, Grace and Stella. Their mum, Annie, was to become like a second mum to me. They were just as crazy as I was and I loved it. They were a poor family with no running water in their house and at first no land line, but I really didn't care. I loved that their house, was in the middle of nowhere and they loved me for who I was. I don't know for sure but I think Annie had an idea of what was going on at home. She is still to this day very protective of me bless her and always tell me straight. Such an incredible lady who takes no shit from anyone. Annie and my mum became good friends too, so it was a nice little circle. Protective, friendly and safe.

I would go over to play at their house a lot. They had so much land, and so many places to play and hide. It was like the

Hogwarts grounds. So many trees, hiding places, so much wild life but no Centaurs or Aragogs in the darkest corners of the forest. It's a shame really because I would have loved a Buckbeak to fly on. Their land was brilliant and somewhere I felt very safe. I would sometimes invite myself over just to get away. Their house was only a few miles away, and no one really asked where I had gone so I knew I was safe.

I don't think Grace and Stella know what was going on at home. My dad was always so nice and loving to other children. Much nicer then he was to me, my brother and sister. He would always put us down. For years my brother didn't think he could do anything right. DIY, or anything like that. He was never good enough for my dad. Only recently has my brother has felt confident enough to try doing things for himself and I have to say when it comes to DIY or decorating, he is bloody brilliant at it. There is definitely talent there.

I remember being in school one day and seeing a teacher, Mr. Scone walking down the corridor with two female students. He was hugging them because they had done something brilliant. He was calling them his two favourite students. I stood there and wished that my dad would something similar to me. All I wanted was for my dad to hug me and tell me he really loved me and that he was sorry for the way he had treated me, but this never happened. After all he was my dad and I loved him regardless of how he was with me. There was one rare night, I remember I woke up screaming after having a bad dream. My dad came into the room and tucked me back up in bed. I will never forget that. It is the only memory I have of him being a real loving father.

Unfortunately, being bullied didn't stop when I left school. When I was twenty I started working for the Co-op in Whitland. At first, I started working in the bakery section and I really loved it. The smell of freshly made bread in the morning was heaven. I'd start work at 6am and finish around 3pm. Then over time I was asked to work on the shop floor as well as the bakery. I didn't mind this at all because I didn't like to do the same routine over and over again. I get bored very easily.

There were a few ladies who worked there too. At first, I became friends with them but then over time their attitude towards me started to change. I noticed little digs here and there directed at me about my weight or the way I looked. I took it on the chin at first but when it was being directed at me every day it was starting to chip away at my confidence.

Around the time I started in the co-op, I started to play about with making jewellery. I would use silver plated wire and twist it around beans and semi-precious stones as a hobby. I created my own website and it started to take off. It was again, me creating things which I found therapeutic. I was starting to hear things from some of the other staff in the co-op about one member printing off pictures of my jewellery and taking them in for the other staff members to criticise and laugh at. Apparently around time, I was the most talked about person in Whitland. Rumours were flying around about my life and I was the victim of bullying from so many. I admit some of this I brought on myself because of my past digressions but most of it I didn't.

Every time I went into work this one person would really bully me so much so that when my dad walked into work one day and I burst out crying. Even though he had treated me so badly when I was little, I was that broken I just wanted someone to hold me. It got too much for me and one shift, I called in sick. I was starting to have panic attacks and dizzy spells. I wanted to lock myself away and hide. I went to the doctors and they signed me off work. I didn't want to see anyone and I stayed at home. I don't remember much about the nine weeks I was off work. All I remember is one of the days I was off, I went outside to say good bye to my best friend Jess who had come to check on me and I saw the main lady who had been bullying me drive passed. I ran straight back inside and grabbed my brown paper bag and started to breath. I was having another panic attack. These people had affected me that much. My friend at the time Meg, told me that this lady, had been spreading roamers I had been seen out clubbing on the weekend in Haverfordwest. At first, I laughed. I could barely leave my house let alone go out clubbing.

My boss at the time Anthony, was really lovely and understanding. He was being transferred to a new store in St Clear's and asked if I wanted to join him. I was so grateful I said yes. Things at the new store were brilliant. I loved it. I was working as an Admin and was training staff and helping the store find its feet. Then the Manager was to be transferred again and a new guy took his place. His name was Craig. At first things were OK, but then after time, I noticed he was starting to treat me differently.

Before Christmas, money was tight. I started to put things from the store aside so when I got paid I would buy them. I put them in my cupboard above my desk so they couldn't be sold. Again, they were still in store and were untouched. One day, money was so tight and we were almost out of electricity. I asked the supervisor that night if we could have £10 credit put on our electric key for our meter as we were being paid the following morning. She was happy to help and put a note in the till that it was to be paid the next day.

Morning came and I went into work. I was called in to the office by the store supervisor and the manager Craig. I was being reported for steeling. No letter had been found even though I saw her write it myself and put in on the desk and another in the till. I was suspended on full pay and fully investigated. I was in shock. The store supervisor was being so horrible towards me in the meeting I just couldn't understand it. What the hell was going on? Also, they had found the cupboard full of items in my office and were accusing me of stealing them too.

Over the next few days, I was just so confused. The panic attacks were back, I wasn't sleeping and I was feeling so down I wanted to hide. Was I to lose my job? How could they believe I was stealing? I told them that the store supervisor had agreed to give me the credit and they said I was so out of order putting that sort of pressure on her. I had a letter through the post giving me a date for my disciplinary hearing in the Kilgetty Co-op store. I looked into what I needed to do to help my case so I felt prepared. When I arrived at the hearing, I met the manager who was to interview me. Once we were in the office he turned to me and said "I've got to be honest Victoria, I have no idea why you are here or how this has happened. Your manager has acted very wrongly and this should never have got this far." I have to say I burst out crying with relief. I was so grateful that it wasn't just me who thought this way. He said that this Craig was a terrible manager and shouldn't have been allowed to do this.

I was given a written warning anyway just because I shouldn't have taken the £10 credit but he fully understood why and was really nice about it bless him. After this I left the co-op and started working at an optician's in town. This was to be my last job I was ever going to have as an employee. My friend Claire, was the manager of The Optic Shop in Carmarthen and asked if I wanted to give it a try as a receptionist. I jumped at the change because it was something new.

I had a three-month trial and was going to enjoy it. I have to say though; I was still licking my wounds from my previous two jobs. My friend new I was dyslexic but because of this I think it made her quite worried I was slip up. I did make mistakes but I think the more I thought about how worried she was, the more mistakes I made. My dyslexia had never been an issue before but this was really starting to get in my way. I was making small mistakes in my spelling but then if someone else made a mistake I was the one who got the blame. It got worse and worse but the final straw came when I had my three-month review. I was taken up to the office and sat down with the owner of the Optic Shop. After a very short time he turned to me and said, "If I had known you were dyslexic, I never would have hired you." Unfortunately, I was the only other person in the room and I had no proof this is what he told me other than my word. I was utterly horrified. As compensation, I was allowed to have a pair of free sunglasses of my choice. I chose a £300 pair that I had my eye on. I went home, and cried. I would never work for someone else again. I had been working since the age of thirteen and my disabilities had never been a problem. I had always found ways round it so for this to had destroyed me.

I don't know why I seem to be a target for bullies, maybe it was because I'm too nice, I don't know. I was an easy target I guess. I didn't have much support at home and felt very lonely. My ex-husband was useless at supporting me. After I was let go from The Optic Shop, I found out I was pregnant with my third child, so in my eyes, everything happens for a reason. I had something new to look forward to and my kids and I were thrilled. My husband, not so much. The reason for his negative reaction, was not to come out till I was seven months pregnant.

# Needing Someone to Love

At aged sixteen, I started going out clubbing. I had made friends with my brother's girlfriend and we would hit the nightclubs together. I started to want more affection in my life and so my first real boyfriend came along, Richard.

Now he was seventeen, so handsome and so loving but I was just so messed up in my own head that I didn't care about anyone but myself. I loved him but not enough to treat him well. Being sixteen, I was so young and as most people know, at 16 years old, you know everything already and no one can tell you differently.

I went out with Richard for about a year and a half. I didn't treat him well and I went behind his back with a few different guys. If there is anything I regret in life, it is how I treated him. If I could say sorry for all that I did I would but I haven't seen him for years. Apparently, I really broke his heart and I'm not proud of that at all.

Just before my relationship with Richard came to an end I met John. Now this guy I really did love well and truly, hook, line and sinker. He was so gorgeous and handsome. Muscly and tanned. Green eyes and dimples to die for. I met him in college while I was studying art. I was seventeen and well, to be honest I was hot and knew it. I wanted John and I was going to get him. Turned out he wanted me too so I ended my relationship with Richard and went out with John. Oh, and I was in love and I wanted him for the rest of my life.

We had been together for about three months when I found out I was pregnant. Not only was I a seventeen-year-old student living at home, pregnant, but my sister, who was also living at home at the time, was pregnant to. We were both due at the same time. It sounds like something from a nasty housing estate but we lived in a very large, four-floored, six-bedroomed house in a stunning village. This was a first for my family.

Now back then, people thought I had got pregnant on purpose because my sister was getting the attention, but I fell pregnant before my sister found out she was expecting. My brother believed it so much he stopped talking to me. I did love attention, and hated being second or hearing the word "No" but this was genuinely an accident.

At first my mum wanted me to have an abortion, but I just couldn't do it. I wanted this baby and I knew I could have it. I loved it already and I couldn't say goodbye no matter what that meant.

Over the next nine months so much happened. I decided to surprise John one day. So, I got on the train in Whitland and headed towards Pembroke Dock, where he lived. I dropped my things off at his parents' house and went to find him. As I walked around the corner of the street, he was kissing another girl, Sam, aged fifteen. I was horrified. I ran back to his house and got my stuff. His mum told me she knew all about it and never thought to tell me. She was a horrible woman. I went so numb. My world had fallen apart. I was pregnant and my baby's Father, was with another girl.

What was I going to do? I called my mum to come and get me because there was no way I could have coped with going home on the train on my own after this. This girl Sam was being given a double bed for her sixteenth birthday and he ended up getting her pregnant at the age of sixteen. I remember hearing the news in college from one of his friends. I had already cut him out of my life by this stage, so I was sort of already prepared. Despite all this, I did however manage to finish college and pass my Art and Design course. I was so proud of myself.

My sister ended up having terrible problems with her pregnancy and her little boy had to be born early. So, Jake was born and he was just so perfect. I fell in love with my new Nephew. Six weeks and six days later my waters broke. With some gas and air and three long hours, Monica Vivian Marie was born. She was the most beautiful baby I had ever seen. She was perfect. I couldn't stop staring at her.

The night she was born I couldn't sleep. I was a mum with my own little baby who wouldn't hurt me or leave me. She was perfect and all mine. I went to find a nurse to ask if I could have something to help me sleep. This was quite normal apparently and she gave me some co-codemol. The next day we were allowed home. When I arrived, I had a huge bunch of flowers waiting for me from my mum and a big banner across the door welcoming us home. It was perfect. I was so happy.
From that day, I was totally devoted to my baby girl. She was everything and my whole life. I had transformed the room next to mine into a nursery but after struggling with being told what to do and with my dad being controlling as always, I decided to move into a place of my own.

My sister had moved out after having Jake and lived in the next village. There was an empty house next door to her, so I moved in there. My parents didn't think I could do it but I did and I loved it. It was just me and my baby girl. No dad controlling me, no stopping me from eating, no restrictions, and no telling me I couldn't go in the fridge. This was bliss. My sister had managed to sort out my benefits so I had money coming in every week.

Every Tuesday, my sister and I would collect our benefits and then go into town to do a weekly shop. We always had so much fun. Over that last year, we had grown very close and this was such a blessing. To this day we are still the best of friends. Our routine was to go food shopping and then take the two children to McDonald's for chicken nuggets and chips. I know it's probably sounds bad but this was the best my life got and I loved it. I was happy and out of danger. My baby was incredible and my best friend. She was everything to me and I wanted to be everything to her.

Over the early months though I started to get really lonely. Monica's father had left me for another girl and she was having his baby. I wanted to spend my life with him, being Monica's father, but clearly that was never going to happen. Yes, my sister lived next door and that was great but it wasn't enough. I felt like I would be alone for the rest of my life.

I remember watching City of Angels one night and after it finished, I went upstairs to my room and I cried so hard. I had never felt so alone in my life. It was the worst feeling in the world. I was never going to find someone to love both myself and my new baby girl. So, this is how I continued my life for a while, believing I was to be alone forever.

After about a year, my sister decided she wanted to live with her boyfriend, Jake's father, in Telford where he was from. I couldn't blame her, she missed him so much but he had to stay there for work. He would come down every other weekend to see Nadean and Jake but being a single mum, this wasn't enough. When my sister moved, I moved too. I found a flat in Whitland so I would be near a train station to go places with Monica as I couldn't drive. Monica and I moved into our new flat at the top of Whitland. It was okay, cold and damp but okay, well for what we needed.

My sister had moved away and was settled in Telford. She was finally happy to be with Jake's father, David and I was really happy for her. Monica and I would walk around Whitland every day. We would take a trip on the train to Carmarthen or Tenby when the weather was dry. We would walk down to the park and play for hours or visit the river running through the town. She was only little so was in a push chair for most of our outings but she loved it.

I was starting to like it being just Monica and me. I was finally becoming happy with my life and who I was. I would get looks from people for being a teenage mum but I didn't plan it, I would have been happy to stay with John but he didn't want me. I did think, if only these people new my story they would think differently. I was a good mum and Monica was always well dressed, well fed and had warm bedding plus she was really loved and very happy.

Our flat however, was not all I first thought it was. The rain would come in through the walls, the heaters were drinking electricity, and during the winter, even a bottle of milk left on the kitchen side would freeze overnight.

I had gone to stay with my mum for Christmas in 1999. When I came home, the flat was freezing. Monica was so cold and it was too damp for us to stay in.

I rang the Environmental Health Agency in Carmarthen and in the New Year, they sent an agent out to examine the flat. They told me that we couldn't live there anymore, and was told to stop paying the rent till it was all sorted. Eventually, it was dry and much warmer after the flat had been updated, but while this was all being done, I tried hard to spend as little time at the flat as possible. As long as my baby was warm, dry, fed and watered I was happy.

Living in Whitland was good for the time being. I was right by the train station, some small shops, near my best friend Jess but on the negative side, I was still the talk of the town. You might be reading this thinking, how could someone like me be the talk of the town? well I was. It was strange. I was only a young single mum living on my own. There were many more like me, but for some reason I was on everyone's gossip radar.

I remember hearing one rumour, that I had a twelve-year-old son at the age of nineteen. This one made me laugh, but the one I didn't like was that I would push my daughter in her pushchair around Whitland or Shitland as it got nicknamed by me later on, as an excuse to sleep with married men around town. Another one was that I went to someone's mothers' house and threatened them in broad daylight because I fancied their daughter's boyfriend. The truth was, I was being stalked by this girl's boyfriend.

I remember after going to the shop with Monica in her pushchair. I was pushing her up a hill towards our flat, but sat on a bench next to the road for a rest. I noticed just down the road this man's car pull over, watching me. He stayed there watching. It wasn't till I got up and walked away some time later that he finally pulled off.

You might be shocked to read this but for me at the time, this was normal, but yes it did frighten me. I remember one night I was in my down stairs flat, watching telly. Monica was in bed asleep. and there were a bunch of drunken men outside my front room window. They were shouting abuse at me. I shut the blinds, but they continued. I remember sitting there thinking if they wanted to, they could have easily broken into my flat because my front door wasn't strong at all. Eventually they left.

I remember when a paramedic moved into the flat above mine, Daniel, I think his name was. One morning I was lying in bed after my boyfriend at the time, Stuart, had gone home from spending the night with me. I looked up in the corner of my ceiling, to see something moving. Then while I was watching, this eye came into focus. It was Daniel in the flat above me, watching me while I was in bed. Thinking back now, he would have seen all sorts of private things, also he would have been watching me changing my little girl. It's horrible to think back now to what he had seen. That day, Stuart bought a can of expending foam over and filled the hole in for me so this Daniel could no longer peep through it.

Honestly, I don't know how Stuart stayed so calm, but then he loved showing me off to people, he loved having a trophy girlfriend so he was probably quite proud. If that had been my husband Adam now, he would have killed him for spying on his girlfriend or wife. Stuart was a coward, so I'm not surprised. Soon after that, Daniel moved away. I started to hate living in this shit-hole of a flat. I know the problems had been sorted but it was getting me down more and more every day. To be honest, from there on, It all seemed to go downhill. My life just got worse and worse with depression, anxiety and feeling like I had no one to trust or confide in. I felt so alone and lost in my own world. The only good thing in my life was Monica, but it wasn't enough and she was too young to put so much pressure on.

# Looking for That Silver Lining

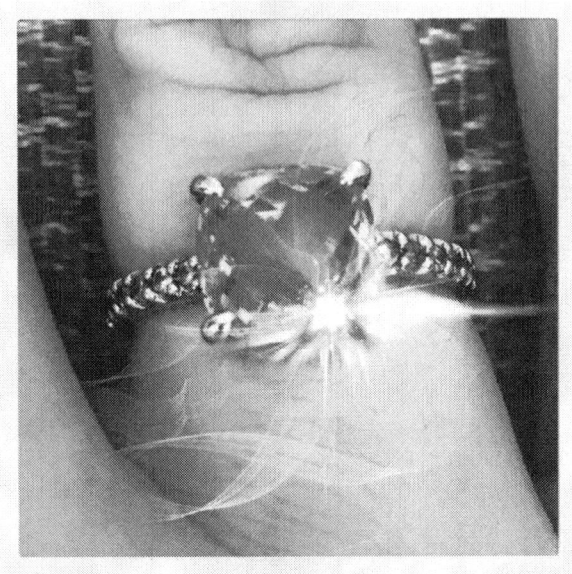

This was the ring I gave to my Mum a few months before she passed away.

Depression was becoming a huge part of my life now. I was getting deeper and deeper into this dark hole with no one trying to help me out. I had no one I could trust. Jess had moved away, Stuart wasn't helping and well Monica was only little so there was nothing she could do. I was needing to stay strong for her. I think this was probably the lowest I had ever been.

I was now on antidepressants, which were knocking me out. Seeing a Psychiatrist one day a week was helping but not fast enough. I went on a downward spiral. Nothing was working. I slept a lot during the day, and wasn't the best mum to Monica. I tried so hard to be, but I just couldn't snap out of it.

I was a big Buffy the Vampire Slayer fan back then. I would focus on that for the time being and would look forward to watching it every week on BBC 2. I remember reading Harry Potter and the Goblet of Fire, but stopped half way through. I just couldn't concentrate.

I think what was really getting me down at the time was my mum had been sent away to hospital after threatening to kill herself by jumping off the bridge in Carmarthen. mum had been sent to Tyler Ward in Carmarthen hospital. In fact, mum was pretty much in hospital for the entire time Stuart and I were together. She was on the phone to a helpline before this and apparently gave some key words that meant she was close to wanting to kill my father. Soon the police were at their home and took my mum to the hospital.

I don't remember much, but I was told things much later on. Again, it was all hidden from me. All I remember was, I had a call from someone telling me mum had tried to kill herself. It was horrible I went into my room in my flat and cried so hard.

Stuart was there this time and stayed with Monica in the other room. How could she have wanted to take her own life? I couldn't understand. What was wrong? What about us? Did she even think about us at the time?

My mum was in the ward for a long time. Then the doctors decided that her and dad were a bad combination so mum was moved to a hospital far away in the east coast of England. I couldn't drive so there was no hope of me seeing her, and dad didn't want me seeing her either. I was shut out completely. By this point, my sister and I decided mum was dead. We were never going to see her again. It was a horrible thought but what could we do? dad had full control and we weren't allowed anywhere near her.

Then mum was moved to a hospital in Liverpool. I have no idea why but this time my dad took Monica with him on visits sometimes, which really lifted my Mum's spirits.

Then one day, on my mum's birthday, my dad went to visit her and told her that he had fallen in love with another woman. He was seeing my mums best friend, Simone. They had become best friends in hospital in Tyler Ward. As soon as Simone was discharged, she made a beeline for my dad. I will never forgive her for this. My mum and dad were not meant to be together and dad leaving my mum was the best thing for her. He was a control freak and didn't help my mum at all, but to leave her this way was just so wrong.

My mum wanted a divorce, but was totally helpless from the hospital. She asked my sister Nedean for help. Nadean decided to get my mum into supported accommodation in Telford, which was going to take what felt like a life time to achieve. Luckily my sister worked in the care section in Telford so had quite a pull in that field at the time. mum after some time, moved into a large house where she had her own room. She was still very poorly, but had a little more independence. She was allowed to go out for the day with my sister or go over to her house for dinner. It was just what my mum needed, but she was still very heartbroken about dad leaving her. She would ring me almost every day from her room asking had I spoken to dad or heard from him. I hadn't and didn't want to. I was furious with dad for what he had done to my mum.

Over time, mum finally seemed to improve. Yes, things were still bad. She was still cutting herself, but she was improving. We knew she would never be back to normal but was getting better and more independent. She moved into a small bungalow, about two years later and had her own car. I was so proud of her. She was doing amazingly and was showing the world she could do it. She was becoming our mum again. I was amazed and so very proud. She was a most incredible woman indeed. My sister needed a medal too because she had worked so bloody hard to help her get to where she was but Nedean did it for the love of our mum. Both were incredible role models and I loved them so much.

When I was living in Shitland, Buffy the Vampire Slayer was my life. I loved it. Much later on, I was to become the owner of the biggest Buffy the Vampire Slayer memorabilia collection in the world. It ruled my life in so many ways. I even named my eldest son after Xander Lovell Harris. When he was born, he was to be called Daniel Stuart Lovell. Again, I loved the story behind Buffy. It was everything to me and what I grew up with, however, I didn't start watching it from the beginning. My sister watched it first, but because I loved the film starring Kristy Swanson, Luke Perry and Donald Sutherland I didn't want to ruin the film by watching the new TV series also created by Joss Whedon.

After my sister nagged me for months about how brilliant it was, and with season two about to air on the BBC, I finally gave in. Oh my God! I bloody loved it and I had only watched the first episode of season two. I couldn't wait to watch the rest. My sister loved it so much that she also named her second child, a little boy after a character from the show. Riley Finn.

Over the years, my life became so hard. I was going through so much with depression, anxiety and stress. Being a new mum again and not knowing what I was going to do with my life. I was also struggling with my then husband, Stuart's family who, since my son was born were treating my daughter very differently. I was becoming more and more depressed. Seeing the way that they were treating my son compared to my daughter was destroying me. I was so hurt because she didn't choose for her real father to leave us. She was the most incredible little girl ever and they just weren't treating her the way they should have been. This also led to a lot of arguments between myself and Stuart because I felt, at the time, he was not sticking up for his step daughter.

When Daniel was two, Stuart and I got married, but I have to confess, on the way to the Registry Office, I really didn't feel like I was doing the right thing. Something wasn't right and I knew it, but because it felt like the right thing to do at the time, I went through with it anyway. Strange really, but a few days after we got married I bumped into Annie, my second mum who said to me... "He'll do for your first husband, won't he?"

Stuart and I met when we were in school, in fact he was one of the pupils who bullied me. Not too badly though, I remember he kicked me because I wouldn't let him borrow my Walkman. So, we had known each other since I was nine and he was eleven, but after being in primary school together, we weren't going to see each other again till I was twenty.

Monica and I were still living in Shitland. We were walking down the road to the shop. I was finally happy with who I was and Monica was still my world. A car pulled up beside me and Stuart asked if we wanted a lift. During the drive to the shop he gave me his mobile number and asked if I wanted to go for a drink sometime. To be honest, at the time, I didn't click that he was asking me out on a date till I got back to my flat. I texted him and we arranged to go for drinks the following Tuesday after he finished Football training.

Whitland was such a small community that everyone knew everyone's business and being a hot, single mum I was on a lot of the boy's minds around the village. So, when I was seen out on a date with Stuart, everyone knew about it and so the gossip started. I had boys coming up to me warning me about Stuart, that he was bad news, and Stuart had people warning him off me, that he was not allowed to go out with me. At the beginning, I had a few guys coming to my flat and yelling at me to go out with them instead of Stuart. Plus, I had ex-boyfriends telling me they regretted dumping me, but at the time I loved Stuart and no one else.

The first time I was introduced to his family was a day I will never forget. We drove to his Grandmother's house in St Clare's. She was a lovely lady who couldn't do enough for anyone. Both myself and Stuart sat out in her garden having tea in the beautiful sunshine while Monica, only about twenty-months old at the time played on the grass. I was getting more and more nervous because I knew his parents and his younger brother and sister were on their way.

When they arrived, they made their way through the house, to the garden. Stuart's mum said hello, but his dad totally blanked me. At first, I thought he just hadn't seen me, but the whole time I was there, he never said a word. If I spoke I was treated like I was something disgusting or I just didn't exist. Monica too was totally ignored and this was pretty much how the next

10 years would continue. I don't know if this was because I was English at birth or because my dad loved to annoy the locals.

One of his main thrills in life was to piss off the people living around him by either complaining to the council about someone's garden or if they were trying to erect a shed, or maybe they wanted to build a track through their own land or paint their house a different colour. dad always found a way to complain about something. It was all to do with who had the power. So, I'm not 100% sure if Stuart's dad was one of those unlucky people. True, this did not give him an excuse to treat me or Monica like shit. I didn't choose him as my father, but at least it explains part of it anyway!

Six months later, Stuart asked me to marry him. I know we were young but I was so flattered that I excepted straight away but years down the line, not long after we got married, things started to go wrong. I wasn't happy with who I was anymore. We lived in a dump of a house, and was so depressed that I couldn't snap out of it. Everything was bad, and I just wanted the world to stop spinning so I could step off for a while.

Things between Stuart and I were not good. He was doing things behind my back and I wasn't being good either. I started to stray and was seeing a guy from where I worked. I think it was the excitement and the distraction that I liked more. I just didn't want to be home. Stuart was treating me like shit and making me feel so ugly that I lost almost all my confidence. So, when I started to see this guy I felt good again, sexy and pretty, but as affairs aren't good for anyone or the people in their lives, It didn't last long. I confessed all to Stuart and I told him everything about what I had done plus who I had been seeing, everything.

It took over a year for my friends and family to forgive me and trust me again. I did everything to try and make up for what I had done, but I continued to destroy myself in the process.

Devoting my whole life to my two babies and Stuart, I just got on with it. I had therapy and did all I could to try and get my life back. This was not going to be easy but I wasn't going to give up.

One of the things I did concentrate on was Buffy and Harry Potter. I had more books to read and I started to collect Harry Potter and not just Buffy. My collections grew and grew, whether it was through presents for my birthday or Christmas or I bought a few items from eBay. I loved having items arrive through the post in the morning. I think at the time, it's one of the things that kept me sane. My Buffy collection was enormous and was displayed all over the front room. What I couldn't display went into boxes and stored in the dining room as best as I could. My Harry Potter collection was very small for quite some time. It wasn't until I lost a very close member of my family years later that my collection would grow into one I was to become world famous for.

As mum was in a good place finally after so many years, my dad was moving away to France with his new wife Simone and I was trying to focus on my life and how I could improve it. By this time, Stuart and I had finished and I was now seeing Adam. My life was very slowly getting better. I was in a stunning house, No longer a shithole in Shitland, And I had my three babies, plus a husband who truly loved me and my babies so very much.

I remember Monica ringing my mum to tell her that our new house in Neath had carpet on the stairs. My mum laughed at this but it just goes to show simple things to others were huge things to us. I was starting to look at things differently.
 Instead of thinking negative all the time and seeing the worst in everything, I was starting to look for the silver lining in

everyday things. Things could always get worse and this became second nature for every day in my life. It really helped. I started to push out the negative people in my life, which in some cases was very hard.

After I moved to Neath with Adam, I would meet up with a few old school friends of mine for dinner. At first it was nice, but at the end of the night, I would head home feeling really shit and down. I couldn't understand it. I remember ringing my mum and telling her. She couldn't understand it either. What was wrong with me?

Over the next few years, there was no improvement. In fact, it was getting worse. I started making up excuses for not meeting up. Why should I meet up for food, when I was feeling so terrible coming home? It wasn't worth it. Over time my best friend Jess, told me I needed to do something with this one girl. Either sit down and talk it through or end it.

So being brave one day, I messaged her and I ended it. I told her that I couldn't be friends anymore which was very hard after twenty-six years. She was one of my oldest friends, but If she hadn't seen by now how she was treating me, then she was never going to see it. I was given some incredible advice once,

"You can't change people, but you can change the way they make you feel".

I cut off our friendship, but started to feel better. Every now and then I miss her, but I remind myself of how she would make me feel and know I made the right choice of cutting ties with her.

Starting to cut out the rotten friendships in my life was really helping. I started to surround myself with positive people, but also people who would give me honest opinions. There is nothing worse than fake friends, or people who make themselves feel better by putting you down. If you know of any, then get rid of them. Trust me this is something you need to do.

I also had the final push when this so called 'friend' had been gossiping about me behind my back. The last straw was when she told my best friend Jess that she wouldn't be surprised if I got myself pregnant, because they were all working full time, and I was bored. By this point, I had enough.

When Adam and I met, I had three children. One of the first things I told him was that if he wanted children of his own, he would need to find another girlfriend because I had three and that was it. No more. I had been thinking of having surgery so that I couldn't have any more children.

You may think it's silly, but after Jess told me this, I decided it was time to have the operation. I took a long list of reasons I wanted this op to the Doctor and he agreed on the spot. Three months later, I had it done and felt so much better. Drastic I know, But I had taken five years to make this decision and I knew it was right. Also, Adam didn't want any more either, so it was the best decision for both of us. I was petrified of getting pregnant for so long, so at least this way I would have peace of mind.

As you have probably guessed by now, I don't like people thinking they know me, or telling me what to do. It makes me more determined to prove them wrong and this is how I am doing so well now. So, after cutting certain people out of my life, finding the joys in every day and focusing on what makes me happy, I feel more amazing than ever. Harry Potter reminds me of this in so many ways. I have surrounded myself in the Harry Potter memorabilia so I can live in it all the time. This is why I collect. It's so I can have it physically here with me twenty-four hours a day, reminding me of who I love and why, my family.

# A Quest for Happiness

Stuart and I had been together for 10 years. Things weren't getting any better and I had found out he had been having an affair on and off for last three years after receiving a message through Facebook from the girl he had been sleeping with. She confessed all to me. This was not a good thing to tell a heavily pregnant woman. Her name was Grainnia and she was a barmaid at the local club Stuart played Football for. She had met me a few times and was pleasant enough. I thought there was something not right as she just kept giving me this look. She came across as very jealous.

One night we went out for a Football dinner and she was there in a yellow 50's style dress. To be fair she looked very pretty. After it all came out in the open, I had people telling me that she had a thing for married men, but as they say, it takes two to tango.

After a few weeks, stupidly, I decided to give Stuart another chance, but he did it again when Harry was about seven months old. This time I finally snapped and ended it. I needed him gone but knew that he wouldn't leave quietly. I told him that he needed to take a few days to himself and that this would do him the world of good. As soon as he left, I messaged him to tell him he was not to return and that it was over between us. There was no going back this time. I felt so much better and like a weight had been lifted from my shoulders.

I remember driving to Carmarthen a few days later and singing 'Good for you' from season 2 of the TV series Smash, at the top of my lungs because I just felt so free. Over the past 10 years, Stuart had chipped slowly away at my confidence till there was nothing left. I would stand in front of him totally naked and he turned away like he was disgusted with what he saw. It got so bad that I would wake up in the morning and put my make-up on before even getting out of bed. I was so low and felt so ugly. Almost like a Dementor, sucking out all my happy thoughts.

There were times when he would show me off like a trophy. He loved me going out in very revealing and sexy outfits. At the time, I liked it too, until that became the only time Stuart would give me any attention.

So many people told me they weren't surprised our marriage came to an end. We were no good for each other, it's just a shame it took us 10 years to realise this. I did get two beautiful baby boys from it. I was again a single mum but this time instead of one baby girl, it was to three babies now. I didn't mind at all though because It was me, rebuilding my life again and my kids were my everything plus I could rebuild my life any way I wanted, so feeling like I could do anything, I decided to go on a quest, a quest for my happiness.

Where to start? Was my new life to be found under a stone, or even in a river? To a faraway land, or just around the corner? I would search high and low till I found it. After all, Harry Potter found his, so what was to stop me from finding mine? I searched for love everywhere, not just for love but for a new me. I would even make an effort while going on one of my children's parent's evenings, because deep down, I had a feeling I would fall in love with a teacher.

Two months later, a friend of mine who I use to work with, invited me to an awards ceremony for a night out. I loved the idea as I needed an excuse to let my hair down. I went shopping a few days before to look for the most incredible Yule Ball gown to hopefully get swept off my feet by a Cedric Diggory or a Victor Krum. I found the most beautiful long, black velvet, backless, dress. My God I looked stunning but I felt so self-conscious. I did my hair into a side ponytail and gave myself stunning dark eyes using my make-up.

When I arrived, I pulled up outside the Stradey Park Hotel in Llanelli and just sat in the car. I couldn't get out, I was so nervous. I wished I could have just apparated into the corner of the ballroom and hide as I hadn't been out in ages and felt so ugly and fat.

Over in the car park I could see some people I knew and because apparating was not possible, I decided to get my ass out of the car and go see them. That way I wasn't going to walk in alone, besides, my happiness could have been disguised in a suit, so for the sake of the quest, I thought it best to investigate further.

We all sat down at our assigned seats. Ten people to a table so the room was full. I got taking to the lady next to me who I hadn't met before. She was the wife of one of the men I knew and was just so lovely. In a way, she reminded me of Professor Trelawney. Her name was Karen and over time was to become a really good friend. Next to Karen was her husband Rob, a friend I had known for a few years, and next to him was a man I had never seen before but he seemed to know everyone else.

This stranger was wearing a deep purple shirt and a dark coloured tie. He had such bright blue eyes and was incredibly muscular. His hair was very short and red. I didn't speak to him at first because we were both fairly quiet. Over the course of the evening, I kept noticing him. He did try to talk to me once and asked about my Buffy tattoo on my wrist, but I got called away to talk to someone else. Towards the end of the night, we were asked to donate some money to charity and were each given a white envelope to place our money into. As the envelopes were passed around, I took note of the name this stranger had written down. His name was Adam.

Adam Maclean, Adam Maclean, Adam Maclean. I kept repeating his name over and over again in my head. I wasn't drinking that night as I had to get home by 12am to the children. It was almost like Cinderella where I had to be home before midnight, otherwise I would change into a servant girl with rags for clothes and my carriage would turn back into a Pumpkin or as the Welsh would say, a leek.

As soon as I got home after checking all was okay with the children, I went straight onto my computer and searched for Adam on Facebook. I found him and sent him a friend request, shame Cinderella couldn't do this, it would have saved her a lot of trouble with her missing glass slipper.

The next morning, I woke up to see that he had accepted my friend request and sent me a message. My heart did a little flutter with excitement. After all it was early days but something was telling me that this stranger would help me in my quest for happiness.

It was my son Daniel's ninth birthday the day Adam and I became friends on Facebook. We talked all day and got on really well. He was the same age as me, a school teacher, and he loved Harry Potter. The problem was I was still technically married and lived an hour's drive from him in Neath. Over the next few weeks, Adam and I just became so close. He was an incredible man, so loving and didn't care that I had three children. Being a primary school teacher, he loved kids. So, in December 2010, I decided to file for divorce from Stuart.

For our first date, Adam took me to see Harry Potter and the Deathly Hallows Part 1 in Carmarthen. I had already seen it the week before with my daughter Monica but being a Harry Potter fan, I had no problem with seeing it more than once. I was so excited. I was to meet him in Carmarthen before heading to the cinema. I remember it was a really cold evening in December and there was a frost in the air. I've got to be honest though, I was so bloody nervous. I hadn't been on a date in over ten years. This was really frightening.

We walked around a little and he was telling me all these stories about what he and his friends would get up to in town. Adam wasn't a local lad but had a lot of friends there. We went for a meal at Frankie and Benny's after the film. I remember he was struggling to eat because he had a problem with an ulcer in his gum.

What if he didn't like me? What if his family didn't like me or accept me? Was I someone he wanted to tell his family about? All these questions were racing through my mind. I was used to not being accepted or talked about for all the wrong reasons so you can imagine how it was making me feel.

Adam wasn't someone I would normally go for, but after my type really hurt me, I decided to take a leap of faith and see if my quest was to be found with him. This wasn't something I could know overnight. It was to be a very long and difficult road but I was not going to leave one stone unturned or one path unexplored. This was my future and I was going to find it. My happiness.

Our first hurdle was that Adam lived 60 miles from me. A 120-mile round trip and he worked full time. How were we to do this? I decided to take one day at a time. My children were my number one priority over my happiness. This I knew for certain.

I had never loved anyone the way I did Adam, but after my first marriage failed, I didn't feel like I could ever do it again. Could I really remarry?

Over time, things between Stuart and I got worse. After all, we had to stay in contact for our children but it was still hard for them. It was a really horrible part of their lives because we were always fighting. I decided I needed to talk to Adam about moving closer to him. Everything about him and his family was incredible, but how did I know this was the right move? I'd have to drag my children away from their father, and to new schools. It was one of the hardest decisions I would ever have to make.

However, over the next few weeks, strange things started to happen. I would pick up the post in the morning and when looking through it, I'd see it addressed to Mrs V Maclean. Then I would look again and it would say Mrs V Price. Before I met Adam, I had a feeling I was going to fall in love with a teacher. For weeks, I was convinced this was going to be a teacher from my children's school. Then one morning, I woke up in my bedroom and looked out of the window. I could have sworn I was looking over Neath. I wasn't, I was in Whitland.

When my Grandmother died on my father's side, I was given a message through a psychic friend of mine, Claire Hickman, that my Grandma knew about her ring I had lost when I was younger, but not to worry, because another one was coming my way. Maybe this was to be my prophecy? A hint to where my happiness could be found? I sat and wandered if there was an orb somewhere in the Ministry of Magic with my name on it?

Nine Months later during the summer holidays and after all the horrible crap from Stuart and his family, I finally moved away to Neath. Adam's dad was rebuilding a house near his family home and it was perfect so we moved in. Adam still lived with his family as I didn't want to disturb the children with a new man for a while. So, for a year I concentrated on my babies and settling them, and me into our new life. We loved it and I loved that we had a fresh start. My kids loved their new schools and made lots of new friends. We would meet Stuart every two weeks in Cross Hands for the children to go and stay with him. He had moved back in to our house in Whitland so the children still had the stability of their old home, rooms and their friends.

Adam and I were on our way back from a night out with friends in Blackwood. He very rarely drank, so was driving. Half way home he stopped the car near a cliff overlooking the black mountains. Even though it was dark, it was still an incredible view. We sat there together, in his stunning Red Celica GT4. We lent towards each other, our heads touching. I remember his hands grasped my head gently and he slowly pulled me towards his lips, kissing me so softly. Then he said, "Will you marry me?" I started to laugh, I was so nervous but new this question was coming. I said, "On one condition, do you promise to always treat me like a princess?" he said he would and then I said "Yes."

My engagement ring was almost identical to the one my Grandmother had given to me that I had lost when I was a kid, so when I got the message from my friend Claire that I was to get another one soon, she wasn't wrong. My ring was utterly stunning. It sparkled so bright. Diamonds and white gold. I truly loved it and still do to this day.

The following August 2012, he moved in to our house and we were one big happy family. Things between Stuart and I were getting better but he was still horrible at times. I remember one time, just after he met his new girlfriend, he rang me to say she was perfect and said she had the kind of body that I used to have before I had our son Dan. This was nothing new but by then it just passed over me. I was happy and in love and was being treated like a princess.

On my birthday, Adam told me he wanted to take me away to Rome for our honeymoon. I had never been abroad before and didn't even have a passport because Stuart and I never talked about going away anywhere. If we did it was to North Wales, or to my sister's in Telford. Adam told me he would take me and I believed him. It sounded so romantic, but first thing I needed to sort out was my wedding.

# A Wizard in Training

My phone rang,

"Hi, is this Victoria Maclean?"

"Yes" I replied.

"Hi Victoria, it's Dana calling from BBC Radio Wales, I think you can guess why I'm calling you ha ha"

"Is it something to do with Harry Potter by any chance?" I asked.

This wasn't the first time I had a No Caller ID call from a Radio or TV station on my mobile, which I feel so honoured about. Since being in the public eye as a world-famous Harry Potter Superfan, I get this whenever there is a new book or movie coming out. I seem to be the go to girl for interviews - which I really love. After all Harry Potter is my life so any excuse to talk about my passion and obsession is always a good one.

I think I'm what you would call a 'conservative' Harry Potter fan. I don't walk around the house in my Harry Potter school robes, or play Quidditch or believe the films are real, I like to be known as a fan who loves everything about the books, films and now the play. I love to find out about how things were created and made, the stories behind the stories, follow what the actors are doing now and also meet fans from all over the world, whether this is at comic cons up and down the country or online through my Harry Potter Collector UK Facebook page. I'm very open minded. I don't care where you're from, your background, your colour, religion or race. I just love all Harry Potter fans. We are like one big happy family.

For me, Harry Potter is about escapism. Being able to forget your own life for a while. It has been a comfort blanket for me through many troubling times in my life so far. For example, when I found out Stuart was having an affair while I was very heavily pregnant, I ended up being in a very big black hole. I needed to switch off so I would put Harry Potter and the Half Blood Prince on loop all night so I could sleep. To this day I thank that film, for stopping me from going insane and miscarrying my baby boy. So, when he was born, he was to be called Harry!

I have been a fan of Harry Potter since I bought the first book back in 2001. I was pregnant with my first son and heard about the new film being released. As I was stuck at home, I decided to start reading Harry Potter and the Philosopher's Stone.

Being dyslexic, I knew it was going to take some time but I was determined to get through it. With my then husband on hand to help with any difficult words, I started to read. It was amazing. Not only was I reading a really good book, but it was my first ever book I had read and also, a book I just couldn't put down. Two weeks later, I had finally finished. I was hooked. I loved it and I couldn't wait to read the next story. Lucky for me, this had been released a few years earlier so I could go to the bookshop and get it.

That is one good thing about me, if someone thinks I can't do something, I love to prove them wrong, and in the past this is all I was told. So, I read and read till I had got to book three, the Prisoner of Azkaban which was to become my favourite. Even though I was three books in, I still wasn't overly obsessed with Harry Potter like I am today. Don't get me wrong, I loved it, but back then for me it was all about Buffy the Vampire Slayer.

Back in April 2007, Deathly Hallows part 1 was in production. Shell Cottage was the home of Bill Weasley and Fleur Delacour after they were married in the Harry Potter series. In the book, Harry, Ron, Hermione, Luna, Griphook and Olivander are captured by the Death Eaters and taken to Malfoy Manor. Dobby comes to free them and apparates them all to Shell Cottage on the outskirts of Tidworth, Cornwall. But in reality, it was a West Wales beach near Pembroke. Freshwater West beach to be exact and it was just down the road from where I lived at the time, so my sister and I took a trip to be nosey.

Arriving at about 8am, we could clearly see something was happening. We could see all the cast and crew trailers, and the production team were getting ready for a day of filming. The weather was amazing and so warm for that time of year, so it was to be a brilliant day.

Over the course of an hour or so, more and more was happening, then David Hayman, the producer of all the Harry

Potter films was walking down the path and looked thrilled to see us. At this time, it was just myself, my sister, and another lady.

Then, our hearts jumped. It was Rupert Grint (aka Ron Weasley) Wearing a thick woolly jumper and just so relaxed walking towards the set. Then I got really excited, Daniel Radcliffe (aka Harry Potter) was walking towards us! Oh my God! I didn't know what to do? I was just frozen to the spot. He was in a blue shirt, and looked very himself, and very relaxed. He smiled at me and I giggled and waved. He laughed ha ha. Then Emma Watson (aka Hermione Granger) walked down the path followed by a large entourage. She had a pair of Ray-Ban sunglasses on, headphones in and a long thick brown bomber jacket. Emma just kept her head down.

We just stood there in shock. The three main characters had just walked past us and they were to be filming right there in front of us. How did we get so lucky? I took so many pictures that day, but my sister, being an incredible photographer took some incredible photos. These photos were to make headlines all around the world.

During the day, we got chatting to the crew. If we were asked to move, we moved and did everything we were told. Over the course of the morning, more and more Harry Potter fans showed up but these people were to be kept away from the set. My sister and I sat down on the grass next to where they were filming and were quiet. I don't think it fully sank it to be honest, we just watched and stayed quiet. The more the day went on, the more we were treated like royalty.

I was bursting for the toilet and one of the crew members heard me. I'll take you to the bathrooms if you like?" he said. We walked up the path the cast had walked down a few hours earlier and he took me to the casts facilities truck. I didn't know what to do, I was so grateful, but then I really did need a wee so went straight in.

After I had finished, I was looking everywhere for the flush handle. I must have been ages, but as I was leaving the cubicle, I noticed a foot peddle on the floor. Thank God, I had found the flush. I washed my hands and went to leave the bathroom. As I opened the door there were two people having a chat at the bottom of the steps to the truck in front of me. One of them was really short. It was Warwick Davies (aka Griphook and Professor Flitwick).

"It's OK, I'm short enough, you can just walk right over me!" he said.

As I walked towards the crew member who had walked me to the bathrooms, I apologised. He laughed. "I did wonder what you were doing? We've had people who have refused to leave, in the hope one of the cast would walk in" he said.

I just looked at them in shock. How could people be so stupid and think that is acceptable? I'm a huge fan but my God, I'm not that stupid! He did panic bless him, but he soon realised we weren't like that. We respected them all as human beings and just doing a job. Besides, we were just so grateful to have been treated to this experience. We weren't about to do anything to ruin that now.

When I got back to where my sister was waiting. She was smiling like a kid in a toy shop. While I had been to the bathroom, my sister was having a camera-off with Hermione Granger. Emma and my sister were taking pictures of each other and laughing about it. I saw the photos and was just in shock. They were amazing. Maybe Emma knew we were not press. They had turned up in droves with very long lenses. This really annoyed us and probably more so because Emma was just doing her job. Wherever she went, there they were. They didn't leave her alone for a minute, bless her.

One of the photographers asked me what they were filming, I was so excited to reply with "Harry Potter and the Deathly Hallows Part 1" He turned to me and said; "Never heard of it".... "Who's Emma playing?" he asked....."Hermione Granger" I said......"Is that anyone important?" he asked. I did reply but nothing I can put on here! I was fuming. I just couldn't understand at the time why they were there being knobs to Emma. For God's sake, she was just a kid doing a job! Now I know it was so they could get the so called 'money shot'.

They moved to film the part on the beach where Dobby dies in Harry's arms. We sat on the beach, out of shot. I had never seen the beach look so clean. Some of the crew had been there the day before picking up all the litter within shot. It looked amazing. After they had finished the shot, Emma was walking towards the beach and the press ran after her. She just looked so fed up bless her. On her way back to where we were sat, she stopped to look at a dead seagull on the sand. there is a shot of this on the internet somewhere, it's quite a sad shot. Walking behind her was Domhnall Gleeson (aka Bill Weasley) and Evanna Lynch (aka Luna Lovegood).

I took lots of photos of Domhnall Gleeson on set in costume, not knowing this was the exclusive The Leaky Cauldron was after, but we'll come to that after.

While my sister and I were sat back in our spot on the set, the crew member who walked me to the bathroom bought us a load of food and bottled water from the catering truck. Plus, one of the security guards for the set also bought us some sun cream, after all it was one of the hottest days of that year. Yep, we ended up getting sunstroke but it was still one of the best days of my life so far.

After we finished on set that day, my sister went back home to Telford and started to edit the photos she had taken. I sent mine straight to The Leaky Cauldron online and told them all about our day on set. They loved it and more importantly, so did their readers.

My photos were everywhere, but then my sister sent her photos to The Leaky Cauldron. Her pictures had over 150,000 hits just on one weekend and they were on every Harry Potter related page, website and were being used as profiles pictures for some fans. Wikipedia also contacted her to ask if they could use some of them for their website.

I am so proud to be able to say we were on a Harry Potter film set. Sadly, it's over, but at least we got that. Now with Fantastic Beasts being released soon, I doubt very much we will be able to step foot on that set quite so easily.

# The Watchful Ghost

I wish I could say that my experiences with ghosts was like a Hogwarts student would have had meeting Nearly Headless Nick or Peeves but unfortunately it was far from it. A lot of you might not know this but I use to be a paranormal investigator. Yes, I know you can laugh, but I had my reasons. This is how Adam and I met. The award ceremony we both attended was the Paranormal Spiritual Awards in Stradey Park Hotel, Llanelli.

My obsession with the paranormal started at a very young age - three to be exact. My family and I went away to spend some time with my Granddad after my Grandmother past away. A few days after we returned from my Granddad's my mum popped into our local shop. She bumped into my father's cousin and she asked where they were living now. My mum replied telling her it was the same house as before. My dad's cousin looked confused. She said she called to the house the other day and an old lady answered the door. When she asked if my parents were home the old lady just looked at her very strange.

My mum was so shocked at this and went straight home to tell my dad. They then called the police, thinking that someone had been in our house while we had been away. The police came and did a door to door around our area. Our neighbours had been asked to look after our house and feed our animals while we were away so mum went next door to ask Cath and Eddy if they had seen anything. Cath replied by saying that one day she had gone to the house and there had been an empty milk bottle left on the door step. Then another day the front door was open. Cath just thought she had forgotten to lock it.

The house was checked over but nothing was missing. It all seemed normal. The strangest part was when the police went door to door asking questions, half the people living around our area saw a caravan in our large driveway. But the other half questioned, didn't see anything. This story baffled the neighbours and the press got wind of it. When the press turned up, they took a picture of my mum outside the house scratching her head. We were all in either school or nursery and my dad was working. When the photo was developed there was a dark, shadowy, figure standing in the bathroom window. Spooky!

A few days later on Sunday evening we were all sat in the front room having tea. I was sat on the sofa in between my mum and dad. Suddenly my mum could smell a really strong smell of bleach. So much so that it hurt her nose but we couldn't smell anything. Then I remember our cockatoo in his cage started to go mental. When I looked over to the bird cage a coat hanger resting on it started to swing wildly. That is all I can remember unfortunately. We never did get to the bottom of it.

This wasn't the only time the paranormal was part of our family life. When I was nine we moved to a small village called Login. The history of the house we had moved to dated back to the sixteenth century. The grounds it was built upon were apparently much older and once were a part of Whitland Abbey Monastery. At some point in its history the building had become a pub. I'm not too sure when but that's the story. Do you remember the man who called me "The Walker" when I lived in Clynderwen near Haverfordwest? Well he once scared me because, not long after that, he asked me had I seen the black ghost in or house yet? Well the truth was, that black ghost had been haunting me for years. Hardly anyone new about it, so when he asked me that it did seriously freak me out. I just stared at him and started to laugh like he was the crazy one. Well he proceeded to tell me about the lady who lived there before we bought the house. Peggy had had a small child and her child once told her mum that she had seen this black ghost on more than one occasion.

My first encounter with this black figure was when I was about ten. I had just completed my first ballet exam at my dance class and my mum told me that I could have one of the black and white TVs as a well done for passing. It was one of those ones you had to twist the dials to get to each channel. Yes, I am that old you cheeky gits! Anyway, the picture wouldn't clear but I kept trying. My brother came to my bedroom door to talk to me. He was chatting away but I wasn't looking up at him. When I did turn to face him, there, standing right behind him was a black hooded figure. He was completely solid. There were no eyes, just a deep shadow.

But I knew it was staring at me. I screamed in terror and it turned and went away. My bother to this day swears that from that moment on, he started to believe in ghosts. My face when as white as a sheet and I just kept screaming. After that night, the sightings became more common. Although this didn't make it any easier. I was a kid and it was so bloody terrifying. I would have nightmares about it. This black figure wasn't just seen by me either. I had my friend Rachel over to sleep one night and she swore I walked out of the bathroom but I was still in the bathroom. After a few years, we realised that there was far more to this house then we first thought.

I remember one night when I was young, maybe around twelve. It was my bed time so I said good night to everyone down stairs and went to bed. I hated going to bed on my own. The house was so big and scary. We lived in a six-bedroomed, four-storied house. The first of which was a very large cellar, the ground floor contained the living room, kitchen and utility room, dining room. The third floor was the bathroom and four bedrooms. The top floor was the attic which had been split into two rooms. The house was creepy enough without the worry of a black hooded figure showing up to frighten me. I used to jump into bed as quickly as I could so I could hide under the covers. I laid there in bed so still because I thought I could hear someone walking around my bedroom. I couldn't look I was too frightened. Then all of a sudden, I felt the end of my duvet lift up to reveille my feet. There was an icy blast of wind as my feet were exposed. Then a few seconds passed and the duvet lowered again. I was frozen to the spot. I couldn't scream or call out, nothing.

Another night I was lying in bed and I could hear what sounded like someone running upstairs in the attic. A child perhaps? Then the sound of a man's voice. Very low, almost as if this person was talking to himself. This went on for so long. Maybe even half an hour. Then very heavy footsteps crossed the attic floor like someone large was walking. The whole of my house and the garden were very strange. We would regularly see people walking into the kitchen, but then there was no one there. Or a time when my dad and I were arguing in the kitchen and we suddenly heard a large bang in the room above, when we went to investigate, nothing was out of place. One Halloween, my mum was throwing a little party for some close friends and children. mum had a rain effect tape playing on the cassette player in the front room where I was. My mum and Sister were in the kitchen preparing the Halloween party food and then they suddenly came running into the front room where I was playing. They looked at me so shocked. I asked what was wrong? Thinking I had done something and they asked me had I screamed? I just looked at them so shocked. I hadn't screamed or heard a scream.

Eventually my father put the house on the market, after my mum filed for divorce. I decided to get a local paranormal investigation team in to find out what was going on. Even though this was years later, living with all that had happened had never truly left me. I would never have been allowed to do an investigation while my parents still lived there. I hadn't told the team anything about the property. In fact, they thought they were investigating the house I lived in at the time, with my children and ex-husband, until I told them, "No. It's my parent's house a few miles down the road."

When we arrived, they started to find their bearings. As soon as we entered my old bedroom the main investigator went into his hands and knees and started to pray. He could feel the presence of a monk. Dressed all in black and that when he did show himself he would always be in very close proximity to myself. Well as soon as he told me this I ran out of the room. I hadn't told anyone except my family about the black figure. According to the investigator, he was named Father Francis and he was trying to protect myself and the other children who used to live at the property with the previous owner Peggy.

He was so sorry to have frightened me and begged for my forgiveness. I was in too much of a state to say anything in return. I needed to calm down. Finally, I did and started to realise that this spirit had been trying to protect me for all this time. There was apparently a spirit that also haunted the house who had killed a young girl before he died. Father Francis was trying to keep me safe from him. This was also the same horrible ghost who had lifted my duvet up while I was lying in bed. we discovered that in total there were nine spirits at that house so it explained all the creepy goings on.

I know your probably thinking what a load of bull shit but believe it or not I'm actually quite a sceptic. I look for the reasons or possible goings on behind it. For example, when we lived in Login, it was in a deep valley. Years ago, there was a train track that used to run right through the middle and in front of our house. Around the same time almost every other night you could hear a distant train coming along the old rail road. If you stood there it would get louder and louder like it was coming towards you. Very scary if you get to witness it. I found out that this is caused by heat. The noise and vibration of the train had been absorbed into the mountain bed and when the air reaches a certain temperature the noise is released. It's the same principal with thick walls in old pubs. The noise is absorbed and at a certain temperature the noise is released. This is often interpreted as ghostly voices. Very clever, Science was also my favourite subject in school.

But I do believe in ghosts, more so now my mum has gone. My mum had a fascination with clocks. Especially broken ones. The night after my mum died my sister, Monica, Adam, Vicky and I were all sat in my sister's front room. Around 1.05am my sisters wall clock started running backwards. Not just backwards but forwards and then backwards on command. We put this down to mum saying one last goodbye to us. God, I miss her.

# A Wife to be Proud Of

"Am I the kind of girl you want to bring home to your mum?" I asked him.

"Yeah!" he replied with a really happy and positive smile. I sat there beaming at him. I had never been told this before. Someone who wanted to bring me home to meet their parents.

It didn't matter to him that I was a mum and English like it had done before. I had lived in Wales almost all my life, so I class myself as Welsh and I'm very proud of it. My family heritage isn't Welsh though. I'm English and French on my father's side and Greek and English on my mother's side. A bit of a mixed race if I'm honest.

Because Adam and I had met on the thirteenth, we saw this as lucky. So, we decided to get married on the thirteenth of December and have a Christmas themed wedding, but we weren't stopping there. An old friend of mine told me that I needed to put a bit on myself into the wedding, to make it about us. Well I took this literally and both Adam and I decided to have a Harry Potter and Star Wars themed wedding with a hint of Christmas too. As it happens, I'm very creative and decided to help cut on costs, I was to make the entire wedding myself, from props, to posies, the table decorations and so on.

I had a year to do it all and I couldn't wait to get started. The only thing I didn't do was the cake, the food, the large Hogwarts Castle that was at our wedding reception and my wedding dress. I made a 6ft AT-AT from Star Wars that lit up and made shooting noises when you walked past it. I did all the Church services.

Our wedding invitations were Harry Potter acceptance letters, with wax seals, and I made a Pensieve from Harry Potter with a dry ice effect machine that spilled smoke over the edges and changed colours. Plus, I did all the jewellery, posies, button holes, floating candles like they have in the Great Hall at Hogwarts and wedding gifts myself. I worked bloody hard but I was determined to make it the best wedding ever.

We got married at our local church in the village which being Christian, was perfect at 1300 hours on Friday the 13th of December 2013. It wasn't planned this way. I wanted to get married at 3pm but because of some of Adams family and their working hours, we had to change it to 1pm. Then we went onto the Bar Gallois for our wedding reception. I have heard from so many people that our wedding was one of the best they have ever attended and even the venue loved it, so much so in fact they ended up buying my table centre pieces off me afterwards.

When I walked down the aisle, I had a stunning piece of music that Monica chose, and when we left the church we played The Weasley Stomp from Harry Potter and the Order of the Phoenix. We did have very large Christmas trees placed here and there and the colour theme was blue and white like the Yule Ball in Harry Potter and the Goblet of Fire.

It was just the most perfect day. We danced to Under the Sea, sung live by a local man Jimi Webb, which was lovely. No idea why we chose that song but it just worked. An amazing friend of mine, Hannah and her husband Matt, made Star Wars chocolates for all our guests as wedding favours and I made a Harry Potter style sweetie trolley like the one for the Hogwarts Express in Philosophers Stone. I had Honeydukes stickers printed for all the sweetie jars, and made my own hand made sweetie bags. We even had a huge jar of Bertie Botts every flavour beans, plus a menu of what to expect in the jar.

After the speeches, one of my bridesmaids, Sam did a Harry Potter and Star Wars quiz. It was just the perfect day. Our wedding cake was a three tier Star Wars wedding cake which was amazing and we cut the cake with the Sword of Gryffindor. Everything was incredible. I have never been so happy.

My father in law Steve even got a little tearful doing his speech. God, I love my in-laws. They are just the best, and love me for me. I have never felt so happy and safe in all my life. I had married the most incredible man whom I loved totally and utterly, and he loved me.

The following May Adam took me to Rome. Flying was terrifying but Rome was incredible. He kept his promise and I had the best time of my life. I had at long last, found my happiness. My quest was now complete.

I had a lot of compliments regarding the props I had made for my wedding. It was even in the local newspaper. I decided to give it a go and make more items. I rented a studio in Swansea where I could call my prop room. I collected lots of recycling material and got to work on a few bits. I was asked to make things like large cauldrons, gargoyle wings and feather fans, but the biggest item I made was to become one of the props I would be known for all around the world.

My husband had started to watch a new TV show but from what I had seen, it was horrible. Violence, blood, rape, sex and incest. I just didn't know what to make of it. It was a period TV show called Game of Thrones. Adam insisted that it was going to be huge and I should try to make an Iron Throne like in the TV show. So not really knowing what would become of this, I set to work.

Four months later in August 2014, my Iron Throne was complete. I didn't think much of it. I thought it was clever that I had made something like this, but it was just a large pain in the ass. I ended up putting it in my shed and there it stayed for seven months until one of my best friends Anthony, posted a picture of it on his wall on Facebook. He then tagged some of his Comic Con friends in the picture.

That day my phone and my Facebook went nuts from people wanting to hire it. Not only that, but while I was making the throne I started to watch the show. I was completely hooked. Over the next eighteen months my throne was to become a celebrity. Not just being in the news but also being celebrated by HBO online, and being used and signed by some of the Game of Thrones cast.

From Kit Harrington to Richard Madden in total to this day we have had over 30 autographs and went from being worth £400 to almost £40,000. Thanks to my Iron Throne replica I now had a celebrity lifestyle. we were in demand all over the UK. Put up in 5* hotels, all paid for. Meeting new cast from the show almost every month. Not only that but I was meeting cast from the Harry Potter films to.

In March 2014, I had an email from Mercury Press asking me if I was able to go on ITV This Morning as a self-confessed Harry Potter fan. Tom Felton had a new one off program going out on the Monday night about super fans and they wanted me and some of my very large Harry Potter collection to go on the show. They were going to send a courier to collect my items to take to the studio in London and then send them back again. All being packed for me and safely travelling up London in their own transportation.

This was on the Friday before we were to go on air on the Monday. During the weekend though, I had already booked a hotel for myself and Adam to stay in Cardiff for Cardiff Film and Comic Con. I booked for two nights at the Park Hotel opposite the Motorpoint Arena, after I found out that Ray Park (aka Darth Maul) from Star Wars was also attending. He was Adams hero and I knew that this would probably make his dream come true.

We arrived on the Friday at about 7.30pm. We got drinks and sat in the hotel lobby. At about 9.30pm, Ray Park walked through the hotel doors in a dark coloured jacket and a rucksack on his back. I've got to say he was bloody gorgeous. He smiled at Adam and I and went to check in. Because we were almost like family with Comic Cons, we had lots of people to see that evening and before we knew it, Ray was back in the lobby getting a drink. Adam couldn't contain his excitement any longer. He asked me if I wanted a drink so used that as an excuse to go over to the bar. I stayed out of the way because this was for Adam and I couldn't have been happier. Over the course of the evening Adam and Ray chatted for ages. Not about Star Wars though and I think this helped. Adam is a second dan brown belt in Karate so throughout the night he talked to Ray about martial arts. The night drew to a close and we went up to bed, to get ready for day one of Cardiff film and Comic Con.

In the morning, we made our way to the lift to head down to the restaurant for breakfast. As we got in the lift, we were greeted by a very friendly, tall and distinguished gentleman. This man was also no stranger to Star Wars fans. It was David Prowse, (aka Darth Vader). Bless him he was a sweetheart, but we had met David a few times before. He remembered us and wish us good morning.

In the hotel restaurant, we sat among names like Jeff Rawle (aka Amos Diggory from Harry Potter and the Goblet of Fire), Kristina Loken (aka Terminator 3), Daniel Portman (aka Podrick Payne for Game of Thrones), Bernard Cribbins and Samuel Anderson (aka Wilfred Mott) and Danny Pink from Dr Who. This was nothing new to us. We were used to having a morning like this when it came to Comic Cons. The trick is not to treat them like a tourist attraction. They are no different to you or me.

The actors were in for a full day of meet and greets with fans from all around the world, so the last thing they wanted was someone nagging them while they were enjoying their breakfasts.

The convention was brilliant as always. I was dressed as The Baroness and Adam was dressed as Snake Eyes from GI Joe. At this point I was size 16 and 13 stone, but I have to say I looked amazing and HOT. I loved it and I felt sexy. Thanks to Adam though, he always made me feel perfect no matter what I wore or how I looked.

What a day. I bought so many Harry Potter items that I just couldn't wait to get back to hotel room to look at them all. After we left the Comic Con, we got changed and went to The Smoke House for food. Our friends Charlotte and Anthony joined us and we had the best time.

Getting back to the hotel we got changed in to nice clothes and heading down to the hotel lobby for drinks with a few friends. What was meant to be a quiet one, turned out to be one of the best nights of our lives. We spent the entire night with Ray Park, getting very drunk and talking about anything but Star Wars.

It was brilliant and we got on really well, so well in fact I ended up getting Ray's mobile number. Nothing sordid though, as he is a devoted family man and very well mannered. He wanted me to tell him when I was going to be on This Morning as he was staying in the UK for a few weeks with his parents. He told Adam and I all about his amazing family, how he was in love with his beautiful wife, Lisa and all about his two children, Rocco and Sienna. What an incredible man. So easy to get on with and has become a friend for life. I got so drunk though that I tried to Facetime him before we want to sleep. I'm so glad he didn't pick up ha ha ha.

The next morning, I was dressing up as Elsa from Frozen. This had become my signature piece because I would dress up as the Ice Queen from Frozen for charity and visit fund raising parties and hospital wards around South Wales for Christmas. I just loved to see the look on children's faces. I was to start doing this more and more as a hobby for a charity called Follow your Dreams.

As we were walking past Ray Park's table in Cardiff Film and Comic Con, he had a mile-long queue of fans waiting to meet him, but as soon as he saw Adam and I he stopped talking to his fans and came out from behind his table to speak to us. This is the kind of guy Ray is. Such a lovely, real and down to earth man. Just perfect.

He asked if we had enjoyed our evening and also to apologise for anything he had done which made me laugh because he was just the perfect gentleman and gave Adam more attention than me as he should.

We ended leaving the comic con early as I had to get back to catch the train to head to ITV that morning for filming live on the show the next day.

My husband and I wish Ray Park

# Surprise

So, with Cardiff Film and Comic Con out of the way, my daughter and I got ready to head to London by train for ITVs This Morning. When we arrived at Paddington station, we had an Addison Lee car waiting to take us to our hotel. A stunning 5* hotel near The Royal Albert Hall. It was all so over whelming. We were taken to our room and it was HUGE. It was beyond posh but because we got to the hotel quite late, we didn't really have time to enjoy it.

Monica and I were starving, so we ordered room service but because this was the first time we had ever had this sort of treatment we ordered everything. It was amazing. Two waiters came up with a trolley full of food and we laid it all out on the floor in front of the TV. In the words of Julia Roberts in Pretty Woman, we were having a carpet picnic.

I hardly slept a wink that night. I was so excited to be on national TV but even more so to be talking about my love and obsession. The next morning, we checked out and waited for our car. One the way to the studios, my tummy was doing somersaults I felt so sick.

The studio was right near the London Eye and was on the Themes. It was an amazing spot. Walking through a prop store room and made our way to an elevator. Then at the next floor, the corridor looked very plain and but at the end of the corridor I could just make out the famous This Morning sofas. Monica and I were taken to the green room and were offered breakfast. The production team were very lovely, warm and attentive.

While we were sat eating our breakfast, a couple walked in with a pushchair. The little boy in the pushchair was called Aidan and he was the rarest little boy in the world. Aidan had

Cloves Syndrome which caused very large and painful lumps all over his body.

Aidan's parents Karl and Vikki were asked to step out of the green room for a minuet as the production team needed to have a chat with them. I was asked if I would watch over Aidan for them. Being a mum anyway, I was more than happy to. Aidan was such an adorable child. He was four, couldn't talk but kept blowing kisses at me. I just kept talking to him over and over again. He was such a sweetheart.

Karl and Vikki had been searching for a diagnosis for Aidan's condition for the last three years and they finally had one. This wasn't the first time they had been on This Morning so were a dab hand at it. After they had appeared on This Morning, they said their goodbyes to us and left. I'm very sorry to say that Aidan passed away just a few months later. Myself and Monica were so saddened by this news and our hearts went out to Aidan's family.

Now I wasn't going to appear on live TV on my own, oh no! They had also contacted a very lovely lady called Lorraine Garside. Yet another Harry Potter superfan. She was almost as obsessed with Harry Potter as I was but Lorraine, collected the books, not just any books, but Harry Potter books in all different languages. She had bought with her some incredible items to add to the set and I was very impressed. I think thanks to that day, Lorraine and I will be friends for life. She's such an amazing a generous person.

Both Lorraine and I were called into the make-up room and checked over. The lady doing my make-up was also a Harry Potter fan and was so excited to show me her wand keyrings she had on her keys. While I was sat there, another make-up lady was just reading out aloud their morning schedule. She read the name Tom Felton (aka Draco Malfoy from Harry Potter). I got so excited and started asking questions.

 Now I don't know if someone behind me looked at her and warned her not to say anything because she suddenly said...."Oh no he's not in today, he's done a pre-recording for the show. Oh, I'm so sorry, did you think he would be here?"

It was OK, I thought it was too good of a day for him to turn up as well. I was told however, that there was a surprise on the day for us too but I thought this might have been it. It wasn't but never mind. I was just so lucky to be on This Morning as a superfan. I mean, how many other fans would have killed to have been invited to do this?

We were waiting in the green room and suddenly Monica started saying mum, over and over again to get my attention. When I looked over, she was staring at something. I followed her gaze and there in the doorway was Tom Felton. My mouth fell open. I tapped Lorraine on the shoulders and she just stood there. I didn't know what to do? He was here, actually here in front of me in the same room. If I'm honest, I did go a little fan girl on him, but backed off when I thought I'd better behave. Tom was so lovely. I asked if I could have a hug, he said "of course you can, I'm not like that other guy!"

He also introduced Lorraine, Monica and I to his then fiancé, Jade Olivia, who played his wife in Harry Potter and the Deathly Hallows Part 2. She was so lovely. I asked Tom to sign my Harry Potter book which he was more then happy to do. Then he asked if he could make anyone a cup of tea.

"Yes please" I said.

After we got talking, I was telling him about my hobby as a prop maker and all about my Iron Throne. He was very impressed and found it funny that it was currently in my front room at home. I told him all about my time on the Harry Potter and the Deathly Hallows set and how well we were treated.

Tom then told me he was going to play golf with Rupert Grint in The Celtic Manor Resort, Newport the following Friday. Yes, some fans would have taken this as an excuse to go and see them but they are people, not tourist attractions. I am only 40 minutes front the Celtic Manor, but I'm not about to go stalking them when all they want to do if have a normal day on the golf course.

Not long after, Gino D'Acampo walked in to the green room. It was so funny because at that moment almost every female was shuffling to get their phones out of their pockets. I laughed but I have to confess I did join in and had a selfie with him, so did Monica. Gino acted like this was the norm bless him.

It was getting closer and closer to our interview on live TV. I was taken to see my items that had been delivered a few days later and they had all been placed amazingly around the set. It looked fantastic, with floating candles, very large book shelf's and cobwebs. I was so excited. Then I got changed in to my Hogwarts robes, all ready.

Now this did confuse some people. I was dressed in Gryffindor robes, but I'm a well-known Ravenclaw. This was because about two months before, My mum, who was a proud Gryffindor, sadly passed away, very suddenly, so I was wearing them in honour of her.

This was it. We were asked to go quietly onto set and wait. Lorraine and I stood there and just didn't know what to do. We knew that Phillip Schofield and Amanda Holden would be talking to someone via video link to America, and then it was on to us. When we arrived on set Gino was making pasta on screen. it smelt so good, and the advice he gave about using a little of the sauce on the pasta before serving. I still do. It looked so yummy. The smell was as close as I was going to get though ha ha.

So, Phillip and Amanda sat on the sofa chatting to Tom about the show he had finished to be aired that night, Tom Felton meets the Superfans. This show was about the craze behind fandoms, not just Harry Potter but the Beatles, Star Trek, Star Wars, Comic Cons, Football and Twilight, trying to understand it for himself. What makes a superfan and why? I have saved this program on my sky box because it was just brilliant. Why doesn't Tom do more documentaries like that?

Suddenly, Phillip mentioned our names, "Come with us Tom, over to the other side of the studio, because we've got Lorraine and Victoria over here. They are super fans. Hello Ladies, how are you?" Asked Phillip. I pooped my pants!

The interview was over before I knew it but it was amazing. My favourite part was where we had to pretend we had never met Tom before, so when he said, "Shall we just hug it out?" I'd like to think that was because we had got on so well in the green room. He was a pleasure and such lovely, warm hearted person.

After filming had finished, Tom came up to me and said how sorry he was that he had spoilt the surprise by coming into the green room before we went on set. He had no idea that he was meant to be the surprise for us. I told him not to be silly, that I was grateful to have met him first. It did make the interview slightly easier. We said our goodbyes, and I started to help the production team pack my items away.

They were all sorted and ready for their journey home, and so were we. Monica and I were taken back to Paddington station for our long train ride home. It had been the most incredible three days of my life. How was I ever going to top this?

# Loss

My mum was a huge Harry Potter fan. Every time they were shown on TV she would treat it like going to the cinema. mum would text me to make sure I was watching too and we would sit there 160 miles apart watching the same film on the same TV channel. So, in October of 2014, I booked for mum, Adam, Monica, Daniel, Harry and I to go to the Harry Potter studios in London.

Bless her, when I had told her what I had done she was like a big kid. She was so excited and was counting down the days till coming to visit. The plan was, that mum came down to us from Telford by train on the 4th of December 2014. The following day we'd head off to Watford to stay in a hotel and then the day after, go to the Harry Potter studios. I think she texted me every day till we were due to leave.

My mum had never travelled to ours by train before and was really excited by this. She asked my brother, Lawrence, to book the tickets but the morning my mum was due to travel she was so nervous. I kept telling her it was going to be ok, that if she had any problems to ask the train conductor or ring us, but once she was on the train, she was fine. We laughed and joked all the way there. She would text me silly things and I'd reply with silly answers. I loved it haha. She sent me a message to say she couldn't have a fag but she had managed to find a tea trolley for hot chocolate. I think by the end, I was more nervous than she was. One more stop to go as she told me they had just passed Port Talbot. I was at the train station twenty minutes early, all ready for my mum. It was so nice seeing her walk off the train. I gave her such a huge hug. I loved my mum so very much. When we got home I made her a cup of tea and we sat out in the garden for her to have a fag.

Now I was pretty strict with this because I didn't smoke. She was to throw the butt end in our garden chimney and that was final haha. To be fair she did. My mum had terrible nerves and needed to know everything plus she had the worst patience in the world. I'd be sat on the toilet for a wee and she would be at the bottom on the stairs shouting up to me, asking where I was and how long I was going to be. She was a nightmare but we loved her no matter what. The night she came down was the Neath Big Switch on. The annual Christmas light switch on. I played Elsa from Frozen for charity events and was asked, along with Monica playing Anna if I could dress up and sing for the event. I was to perform on stage to 500 people and then Santa would be switching on the lights. It went brilliantly and we sang beautifully.

After the performance, we were asked to do photos with the children and once the last child had passed through, my mum picked up the train for my dress and ran off with it. The problem was I was attached. This was her way of making sure I was leaving to head home. It was so funny and we couldn't stop laughing. She just kept saying...."quick before another child spots you!"

Finally, we got to the car in the Morrisons car park next to Neath Castle. We got home and got sorted, ready to leave in the morning for London. I don't think any of us slept well that night because we were so excited. It was to be mums and my kids first time at Hogwarts in the Snow. Between the end of November to the middle of February the entire Harry Potter studio tour was decorated in Christmas style props from the film. This consisted of twenty foot Christmas tree in the entrance hall and the Great Hall, snow in Diagon Alley and the entire miniature of Hogwarts castle covered in snow.

This is actually salt and takes four days to put on the castle using sieves and a cherry picker. The whole of the studios is closed for these four days to do this and to decorate the studios in some of the most incredible Christmas decorations used in the films. This is also the time they do their staff training and anything else needed while the studio is closed to the public. If you haven't been already, you need to go because it is the most incredible experience I have ever been to. I have attended five times now and I plan to go again soon. While we were at the studios we did so much. It was brilliant and mums face when she saw the snow was a picture.

When we had finished the tour, I bought myself a stunning solid silver necklace with Harry Potter's acceptance letter silver charm attached. It was not cheap but I loved it. My mum loved it too but then she loved everything Harry Potter. One the way home we talked about all we had done and seen and we were all just so happy. mum just kept saying thank you for her amazing Christmas gift from us. This was to be the last trip I was ever going to take with my mum. On January 22nd, 2015, almost two months later my mum rang me to tell me all about her day. She told me that her and my sister had been shopping in Asda. Then they had gone back to my mum's house and sat and chatted for ages about everything and anything. I had just stepped out of the shower so was standing there dripping wet in a towel.

"Hi Mum, I said. I'm standing here naked, I've just got out of the shower"

"Oh sorry Darling, I didn't realise" she said.

"It's ok mum, it's not your fault. I love you and I'll talk to you tomorrow," I said.

Mum ended the conversation with "OK darling. I love you too. Bye"

This was to be the last time I would ever hear my Mum tell me she loved me. That night, only three hours later, she died in her sleep. My mum was found the following day all wrapped up in her bed, in the blanket she knitted all cosy and warm fast asleep in bed, but this was a sleep she was never going to wake up from. Adams phone went off, it was a text from my brother. All it said was, try kicking the door in! Then about twenty minutes later, my sister rang my phone. "Vics, where are you?" She asked me, her voice shaking.

"I'm at home. Why?" I asked.

"Where are the kids?" she asked me.

"They're here" I said, getting a little worried now.

"You need to go somewhere out of the way. I have something I need to tell you"

So I went into the next room and Adam followed.

She said, after a long pause "Mums died." I just stood there.

"She couldn't have. I was only talking to her last night. Don't be silly, no she hasn't" I broke down.

I didn't know what to do. This couldn't be real. How could she not be here anymore? No, she was still alive. This must have been a mistake.

My friends Charlotte and Anthony were visiting at the time and I didn't want to upset them. I asked Charlotte to come into the room.

In an almost shocked and unbelieving voice I said shaking "Erm, my mums just died. I need you and Ant to go if that's okay?

"Oh my God Vic, are you ok? Is there anything I can do?" She asked. To be honest, at the time it all seemed like a film or something. It wasn't real and everything felt like a dream. They left and I told Adam that we'd have to go to Telford first thing in the morning for me to see mum for myself.

Adam said, "Forget that, you need to be with your sister now!" He through a few of my clothes and things into a bag. The kids went to Adams parents and Monica came with us. On the way, I couldn't concentrate. I just stared out of the car passenger window and switched off. I think that was the only way I could of coped at the time. Then suddenly we saw a flash of white. Adam had run through a speed camera half way to Nadean's. I don't think he was going fast but a little over what he should of been. When we got to my sisters, I didn't know what to think. My sister had split up from her husband the year before and was living with her new partner, Vicky. I hadn't met her before so this was strange. I was happy to see my sister happy though and looked after by her then girlfriend. She was a lovely girl and loved my sister so very much. I just hugged them both but I didn't cry.

We tried to keep that night light hearted. We told stories about my Mum and the crazy things she would do. Believe me there were so many. We laughed so hard that night, but then we would realise, Mum had gone, and we would go quiet again.

I felt numb. It wasn't till we went to see my mum the following morning that it finally hit me. My mum was in the hospital morgue. We were asked to sit in the waiting area for them to get my mum ready for us to view her. We went in one by one. When it was my turn, my sister asked if I wanted her to come in with me.

Now in my family, we do things a little differently. After all we have been through, we like to make a joke of things. Before I walked in, my sister said, "now mum just looks like she's asleep, and has put on a little weight".

I laughed, and thought I was OK to go in. Adam walked in beside me and I went in to the room. It was really cold and dark. There was a police woman stood in the corner of the room. This was slandered procedure when someone dies suddenly. I said hello to her and looked towards my mums body. I saw her laying there with her eyes closed and her knitted blanket over her and I just broke down.

I fell almost to the floor. Adam and my sister caught me. The police woman got a chair for me and helped me on it with them. I don't remember much after that. I just remember kissing her head over and over and thinking how cold she was. I touched her cheek with the top on my finger as if to wipe a tear from her face. Her cheeks were normally really warm and full but it didn't move. It was starting to go stiff with rigor mortis. I kept telling her I was so sorry because I didn't keep her on the phone for longer or phone her back the following morning. It wouldn't of made a difference though because she died a few hours after I spoke to her. We left the morgue and drove to my mums bungalow.

She lived just a few miles from my sister in a small one bedroom, supported accommodation bungalow in Stirchley. Just perfect for her and her little Chihuahua, Fifi, with a small front and back garden. mum needed supported accommodation because of her mental health and also because my mum had early signs of dementia. Her memory was just terrible. I remember a few years ago, she went to see Harry Potter and the Deathly Hallows before it was released in the area, as a treat for her and my sister after the success of the photos my sister had taken on set.

A few days later, my mum went to see the film again and couldn't remember anything about it. There wasn't much mum could remember about our childhood either. I would ask her questions such as "do you remember this mum?" and bless her, she just couldn't. I think it got very frustrating sometimes, and sometimes, she would ring me and cry because she couldn't remember if she had done something or taken her tablets or not. It was heart-breaking. When we arrived, at my Mums bungalow, my brother was already there sorting through my mums things. He took over everything when it came to the estate and my sister and I were grateful for this. Mum didn't have many valuables, so it wasn't too worrying going through her belongings.

When my mum and dad divorced, my mum was in hospital and because of this, my dad pretty much sold everything my mum owned and kept the money. Even items she had inherited from her own Mum. I however, managed to rescue my Mums wedding and Engagement ring, after dad had told mum the hospital had lost them. They hadn't, he had locked them away in a box in his room. When I told mum that I had found them, she said she wanted her wedding ring but wanted me to have her engagement ring.

Now ever since I was little, I wanted this ring. It was an aquamarine solitaire with a yellow and white gold band. It was stunning. The shank part however needed repairing because it was very thin, so I sent it off to be repaired. when it came back I loved it. I wore it all the time. Bless my mum for giving me this however I finally gave it to my sister when my then, husband Stuart bought me a very large, 3ct princess cut solitaire and diamond ring for our anniversary, but after Stuart and I divorced I gave this ring to my mum as she had admired it for years and I couldn't face looking at it anymore.

She was over the moon when I gave the ring to her. She promised to never take it off. I made a joke and said but when you die, I want it back! I didn't think I would be getting it back that soon. When mum passed away, the ring came back to me, but sits on my mum's ashes, in my house, so she still has it sort of. I'm sorry to say that I just can't wear it. It's strange but ever since I've had it back, it just feels so uncomfortable on my finger.

While at my Mums bungalow, my brother told my sister and I that there should be nothing left of value in my mum's bungalow due to burglaries in the area. I wanted to take everything, anything that belonged to my mum. The idea of things being thrown away was heart-breaking, but because it was supported accommodation, we only had two weeks to clear it out before the next lot of tenants moved in. It was heart-breaking to think we had a timeline but it was reality. Normally you only get one week, but because mums death was so sudden, we were given two weeks. The amount of Harry Potter items was quite amazing and naturally they were given to me which I felt was very heart-warming, but still painful. I took the hoover because my brother and sister had recently bought one so I took this one home. I had jumpers of my mums, some of which still smelt of her, and also blankets, teddies, all her jewellery, which is still in a carrier bag in my house. I haven't had the heart to go through it yet. I came across so many photos, diaries, painting my kids had done for her.

Plus, a Harry Potter DVD box set that she asked my brother for, for Christmas that was still sealed. When my brother saw this, he cried. Her fridge was full of sweets. She loved toffees covered in chocolate, but having false teeth, she just sucked them. Her kitchen window sill was covered in Orchids plants that we had bought her over the years for her birthday or Mother's Day. I wanted everything but I couldn't fit it all in my car. I didn't care what it was, I just couldn't cope with the idea it was to be thrown out. When we left, my car was full. Blankets, pictures, paintings, drawings, hovers, clothes, jewellery and a lot of Harry Potter items, such as bins, cups, scarfs, books, badges, postcards and magnets. I didn't want to drive away though.

Mum was going to come back wasn't she? was this all real? It really didn't feel like it. It felt like we were acting out a play almost. That we were just playing a role. Since losing her I have become more and more obsessed with Harry Potter. I need it more than ever now. When I hold something from JK Rowling's Wizarding World, I am just that one step closer to my mum. I feel her around me, watching over me and I know that everything I now own, she would have loved. It is an obsession and one I don't think will ever go away. I hate leaving the house without wearing something Harry Potter.

My Hogwarts acceptance letter necklace means the world to me but it was the last thing I ever bought while on a trip with my mum. It just so happens we were at the Harry Potter studios and it's a Harry Potter necklace. When my Granddad passed away in the September that same year. Because he left me some money, I decided to buy the matching charm bracelet so would always have him with me too. He died age 101 so not a bad age at all. He was an amazing man Frank and was truly in love with his whole family. Just like we were with him and his daughter, my mum. I still feel bad for not keeping her on the phone for longer that night. She was always there for me no matter what she was going through and would always answer the phone when ever I rang. She was my best friend and someone I told everything to. She was the best mum ever. After her funeral, I had the ashes into glass white gold rings made for both me and Monica so I could have her with me always. She is also in a small glass jar by my bed and every night I cuddle one of mum's old teddies. Mum was everything to us. I loved her more then I could express and we were so very proud of her.

My Mum with my baby girl Monica

Mum I love you Always xxxxx

# My Bestie

"Come on woman. My God you would be late for your own funeral!"

Jessica Nickels, or Summers as she was known by, has been my best friend for as long as I can remember. How she's stayed my best friend I'll never know. She's put up with so much crap from me it's unreal. I think only Jess and Adam truly know the real me. I met Jessica in school. She was in the same year as me but we weren't in the same circle of friends. In fact, we never even looked at each other. When I was fifteen I started going out with her brother Lee. This didn't last for more than a few weeks but after we finished, Jess and I started to get to know each other.

At first, it was a love hate relationship, as in she hated me but over time and after painting a few bedroom walls things slowly started to change. We had quite a lot in common but then we both lived in a village where nothing happened so that was the first thing. We both loved horses and animals and we both had annoying and hard to live with family members. That in the eyes of "Shitland" was as they say, a match made in cow shit, just like Jess's farts.

Over the years, Jess and I have kind of just put up with each other. Well her more than me. I remember one time my mum was throwing a party for my father's 50th and I was allowed a few friends over. Jess came along but I think by the end of the night she really wished she hadn't. My brother thought it was funny to dare his little sister to down a large glass of Harvey's Bristol Cream Sherry. Being fifteen, and wanting to look cool, I did! As you can expect, I was sick all over my next door neighbours house.Jess took my up to my bathroom, stripped me off and hosed me down with the shower head. I don't remember much other than that really. The next day I was told that Jess was not to speak to me again plus I had really made a terrible impression on her parents who, to put it mildly were not too happy with me.

Jess has been there for me more times than I can count. I owe her everything for all she has done for me. Even when I've been the friend from hell she's stayed by my side. When my mum died, she rang to tell me she didn't think she was able to attend my Mum's funeral with me but what I didn't realise was, she felt broken too for losing my mum but because Jess would do anything for me no matter how hard, she turned up and pretty much carried me through the service. If it wasn't for her I would have collapsed on the floor.

Watching my family carry my Mums coffin broke me. I couldn't believe that was my mum. I just kept repeating it over and over again. "My Mums in there" Jess walked me through the service that my Uncle Paul was doing as he's a priest. My sister and I managed to sing "In the Arms of Angels" during my mum's service. I was ok because I managed to switch off and focus but my sister really struggled emotionally. Afterwards I sat down again next to Jess and she held my hands. I just kept looking up at my mum's beautiful coffin in front of me covered in pictures of butterflies and waterfalls. After the service Jess and Karl left. How Jess stayed so strong

I'll never know. We're like family. I love her so much. I don't think I tell her that enough. We've been so close for so many years that we are like sisters. I love her so much.

We have a funny way of dealing with things though, we always laugh. Jess has a mouth like a sewer. It's so funny and has the worse farts in the world. The night before my wedding, Jess was my maid of honour and was staying with us. We ordered a KFC bucket for dinner and had wine. Well that night she was sleeping in my boy's room as they were staying with Adams parents that night. Jess had the worst wind ever. It was so bad we could smell it with the bedroom doors closed. It bloody stank. Jess was using Monica's Miley Cyrus duvet covers and I swear har face on the covers turned green she was that bad. She will hate me for writing this but its so funny.

When I lived in Shitland, Jess and my friend Rachel moved into the flat next door for a short period of time. It was just the funniest time ever. I remember one night Jess and I decided to go for a walk at 2am in the morning. Monica was staying with my mum and dad for the weekend so Jess and I felt adventurous. We went for a very long walk, pulling all the shrubs and weeds and all sorts of things from the surrounding gardens and pathways. Every time the police would drive by, we would through our jackets over our pile of shrubery. No idea why we felt the need to do this but this was our life in Shitland. At least we weren't out getting drunk or taking drugs. This was as wild as it got for us.

Monica loved and still does love her Aunty Jess. Jess would drop anything to help her as she calls her 'surrogate daughter' and Monica sees her Aunty Jess as her second mum. I love that they are this close. It's truly amazing. I know that if anything happened to me, Jess would always be there for her.

You know that relationship you have with someone, where if you don't see them for ages, when you do finally meet up it's like no time has passed, well that's us. It doesn't matter what I've done or what she has done, we will be there for each other till the end. I really love you Bob xxxxxxx

Jess and I at Mell's wedding back in 2000

My bestie is the best in the world

# A Deep Dark Hole

Photo taken by Jon Williams of Port Talbot

Sometimes, I sit on my bed feeling so down. Like I've lost something but I can't explain what it is. I sit down in front of my mirror, not looking at myself, but the floor upon which I sit and stare feeling like I could never smile again. This I put down to having depression.

People who have never suffered from depression will not understand. Some think you can simply snap out of it but it's not like that. Imagine your digging a very large whole, deeper and deeper in the ground because you thought it was your only way out. Then you simply stop. Look around and then up at how deep you have dug, and your stuck at the bottom with no way out. Then it gets darker and darker, colder and colder as the night draws in. This is depression. JK Rowling gave depression a form in her incredible Dementors. The guards of Azkaban prison in her Wizarding World of Harry Potter.

I've suffered with depression, anxiety and panic attacks for as long as I can remember. I'm on anti-depressants but this is more for my hormones as I started going through early menopause at a young age. My mum was thirty-two when she started, I was thirty-four. I'm OK with it though, because I've had my beautiful children. I don't want anymore. In June 2014, I had the snip. I knew the day I had Harry I wouldn't have any more but because Adam has never had any children of his own, I could never ask him to have the snip. If anything happened to me, He can still go on and have children of his own if he wanted.

After Harry was born so early, and with us almost looing Dan when he was six, it's so hard to be a parent sometimes. Just after Dan turned six in December 2007, He developed a cough. Six weeks later we were rushing him into hospital with a collapsed left lung. He had pneumococcal meningitis. He was on life support to help him breath. It was so scary watching my baby boy fight for his life. After about six days, things started to look good, but just before the doctors came round to see him one morning, I noticed he couldn't sit up straight and I was telling him, "Come on," I said, "You might be able to go home". What I didn't know was that Dan had got worse. His lung had collapsed again but this time, nothing the hospital could do would be able to help. He was rushed to Cardiff hospital for an operation. The wall of his lung was full of infected fluid. A boy of Dan's age, would normally have about 30mls of clear fluid around the walls of his lungs. Dan had over 1230ml of infected, chewing gum like, fluid which was slowly suffocating him. He had developed pneumonia, pleurisy and empyema.

Dan was so poorly that he had to have a chest drain fitted. He couldn't walk, sit up straight, smile or laugh. He told me he wanted to give up and end his own life. Dan would lay there in his hospital bed and tell me that Monica wouldn't let him play with toys, but Monica wasn't there. She was staying with my sister Dee in Telford. The fluid on his brain caused by the Meningitis was causing his to hallucinating. He would realise that Monica wasn't there and burst out crying. It was three weeks of pure hell. Watching my baby boy want to give up and die. All I could do was be there with him. I would read him chapters of the Harry Potter books which he loved. He would ask me to. He hated seeing the other children play and he was stuck there, not even being able to smile or have a reason to.

Over time, and with a lot of help from friends and family, Dan was on the road to recovery but what we didn't know was Dan would end up with brain damage. No one was to fully know this until years later when his brain would develop more through age. After Dan had recovered enough to have the chest drain removed and was finally allowed home, it was the 23rd of December and the house was nowhere near ready for Christmas. I didn't care because I had already had the best Christmas present ever. Dan was home and on the mend. I was so happy. He was still very poorly and because of the severity of his illness, He was prone to more infections. Dan was on antibiotics constantly for about six months. He suffered with fluid on the lungs so we had to hit his chest every morning and night to help it come up and out of his lungs. He was on very strong steroids, to help him breath and for a few years was still very poorly.

The illness effected his mental state too. He was so naughty and couldn't talk about his illness at all. It was so hard but we tried to get through it. In 2012, we were told that Dan had brain damage due to the Meningitis. He was diagnosed with ADHD.

This was a breakthrough because I knew deep down there was something not right. So, to finally be told that it wasn't in my own head, that there was something wrong with my son, was a relief and we were finally able to get him the help he needed.

Dan is now 15 and so intelligent. He's in year 11 at school and is on medication, but only during school time. This is his own requested, so he could, in his words, shut his brain off and concentrate. Having ADHD used to be difficult for him, but now thanks to his medication, and very limited time on game consoles, he can concentrate on his school work. He's an incredible child who loves his family so musc. He is so devoted to his mum and hates the idea of disappointing me bless him. He's an amazing big and little brother and an incredibly gifted son to be proud of. I love my babies with all my heart.

All three of my babies make me proud. I'm so very lucky. Having depression means that being a mum is hard sometimes but you try to get through it as best as you can for them. They don't understand and they can't help you so you try to carry on. Luckily for me, my kids are amazing and understand when I'm struggling. I have a pair of ear muffs that I wear if things get to much for me. They know when I put these on to just give Mummy a little space and not to argue with each other. They do some housework and they just let me have my space until I'm feeling myself again. This doesn't happen very often, maybe once a month. I'll wear them if I'm struggling to cope. I find it calms me down.

Yes, you might be thinking I'm crazy but I don't care. We all have our coping mechanism, this is mine. People don't know it but I have slight autism and ADHD. So does my brother and sister so we do have our own way of coping and for us, it's the best way.

I never know what will set me off my depression though. I could wake up in the best of moods, but then something could happen and that's it for the rest of the day. Lately it's been because I'm seeing Christmas stock in the shops and it reminds me that this will be the second Christmas without my mum. It was her favourite time of year so it is going to be hard. I haven't cried for a long time and I still find it very hard to cry. To be honest I can't remember the last time I did. Oh well I'm sure it will come when it's ready. I don't like it to affect my family. It's hard but they say you take it out on the ones you love.

One event that really set off my depression happened last May. As Charlie and I dressed up as Elsa and Anna for charity events, we were approached by Margam Park. They were putting together a superhero event in the grounds to raise money for the park. Charlotte and I were asked to perform and sing as the characters from Frozen. We were so excited about this. My daughter Monica was going to be dressed up as Olaf and we had a huge performing area just in front of the main castle outside. The weather was incredible. They were expecting over 8000 people to attend but actually over 13,000. At the time, we didn't know anything about the shear volume of attendees. We only saw what we had in front of us. Crowds and crowds of people, children, parents and older people. It was amazing. When we were not performing we were trying to meet as many children as we could and loved every second. Again, we were not paid for doing this. It was purely for free and for a good cause.

Towards the end of the day, I finally saw my husband. He looked terrible and so drained. Turns out that the day outside of our little performing area wasn't as well met as we thought. There were to many people for the park to have coped with. It was crazy. It got so bad that there weren't enough toilets for the visitors. There was a seven-mile queue to get in to the park from the M4 and the police were called to assist. Not only that, But the bank holiday traffic had also got court up in it to. A lot of people blamed the park but to be fair, but it was unprecedented at how many people turned up. We had a brilliant time. I love meeting the children. Their faces just light up when they see their idols in front of them. They are simply star struck. When the event was over, we cleared up and went home. I was so tired but beaming from the most amazing day.

We were so happy to have been a part of such an incredible event and had some lovely feedback from parents we had met throughout the day. The next day, I had a few notifications on my phone. It was news articles about parents complaining at the organisation of the event. I was so shocked but thought you can't please everyone. We didn't see the negative side of the day from where we were. I was contacted by a few people saying that our performance was the only one worth seeing. This was lovely and I still had nothing bad to say but this was soon to change.

# A New Me

This was the picture that got so much negative ettention.

After a few days, I woke up to loads of texts and Facebook messages on my phone. So many people saying, "Oh my God Vic, are you alright?" "Those comments are bang out of order". I was just stunned. What were they talking about? I went on my phone to see I had been tagged multiple times regarding a news article. What the hell was going on?

*"Stinking toilets, massive queues and £19 to see shoddy Olaf: Parents fury at 'rip-off' Frozen fun day which featured dodgy costumes... not enough superheroes."*

The first picture that greets you as you look at the article is a photo of me as Elsa Underneath it says....

*"The Frozen Show - one of the only events to take place outside the castle - featured 'Elsa' wearing a green dress and flip flops"*

I was wearing the 'Elsa' summer dress from their short film 'Frozen Fever' which as Frozen fans knows is a green dress covered in flowers. It is a stunning dress and my favourite out of the two. I Was wearing flip flops because we were on the grass which was very soft. My Elsa shoes are simply stunning but high heels covered in Swarovski crystals were so not suited for the grass.

Being in the public eye makes you a target for this sort of thing but I was not prepared for what was to come. Below the article was the comments section. Oh boy was I in for a shock. All 1.1K of them. The shocking part was that around 40% of these comments were directed at me personally. Here are some of the comments:

Geegeebg from London wrote *"Is that really a woman"* I *wonder???? Why would you actually want to go to an event like this? You know it's going to be c\*\*p before you even get there"*

Liz-318-13 *wrote "Let it go....let it go....let it go... 'And boy, did she let it go!*

Arkley xxxxx wrote *"That 'Elsa' looks like a painted docker in drag, poor kids, poorer parents"*

Paloma wrote *"That singing Elsa looks like a bloke in drag - ha ha!"*

Wastedandwounded *wrote "Ha ha. More like Elsa's Nan!"* comments on this soon continued with Sir Bob writing "haha was just about to type the same thing... *Off down the bingo after this"* Then Miss Shirley wrote *"Nan??? more like Grandfather".*

Laurel *wrote "A fat 45-year-old Elsa in flip-flops. Good lord. The organisers should be ashamed"*

Stevoid wrote *"Looks like Elsa spent a lot of time learning her part in Frozen .. by hanging round the fridge"*

lovestosew wrote *"Loling at the porky Elsa in the cheap flip flops"*

They got much worse but to be honest. I'm sick of looking through them. There was this particular one that said, "When you've finished with that dress, can I use it to cover my pool table?" It just ruined me. I stayed locked away in my bedroom for the rest of the day. If you want to see them for yourself, just google the headline. They are still there for all to see. I felt so bloody fat. I wasn't huge though, I was a size 16/18. This to me at 5ft 5", isn't big. They were just jumping on the band wagon looking for someone as a target but try telling me this back then. I was broken and so hurt. I hadn't felt this ugly since I found out Stuart was having an affair.

A few days passed and I decided to do something about my weight. I was stunning and needed to know it for myself. So, I contacted the only lady I knew who could help me. Donna Jones from the Ynysygerwn Cricket Club Slimming World near where I lived. She was amazing and was there no matter what. I told her what had happened and that I wanted to join. I was broken and needed help getting me back to who I was. I didn't want to be a size 8, I just wanted to get me back again and if losing weight was how I was going to do it then Donna was my girl.

Tuesday morning came and I was so nervous. I drove to the cricket club for about 9am after I had dropped Harry off at school. I sat down with a few other ladies who were also joining that day and listened. Donna was just so lovely. She made everything sound so brilliant but it was a lot to take in that day. How could I be allowed to eat all that and still lose weight. After our new members talk I was weighed. 12st 10lb. That's not as bad as I thought but still not where I wanted to be. I wanted to get to 11st to still be curvy but also slim enough to go shopping wherever I wanted.

Not long before the Margam Park incident I ordered a new blue Elsa dress for the winter as Charlotte and I had been asked to sing to hundreds of people at the Big Christmas Switch On in Neath. When the dress arrived, I knew it was too small by looking at it but it was meant to be tailored. Instead of sending it back I thought I would try and loose the weight. There was at least a 2-inch gap where the dress was meant to meet.

After being with Slimming World for three months, the dress finally fit. When Adam went to do it up he said, babe this isn't going to fit, and then the zip went all the way up.

I was screaming "Monica, Monica" because I was in utter shock. When she ran up the stairs I said, "Look" I said and I turned around on the spot to show her. She was so thrilled. Adam was holding his ears because I was screaming so high pitched. That was after losing half a stone. Now I was lost a total of 1 stone 9lb and am a healthy size 10. I'm so proud. I still have a little was to go yet but my God I feel amazing.

Victoria in a national magazine

I sent the story to the newspapers because of what it had done to me. I was so pleased. The title of the press clip was "Elsa has Let It Go" and I couldn't be happier. I'm a new woman and all my old clothes had to be given to charity because nothing fit me anymore. I owe Slimming World so much and for the way I look now, I am so very, very happy.

Victoria going from as size 16/18

To a healthy size 12

# The Inspiration

Since finding who I truly am with huge thanks to the people in my life and must importantly my children and my husband, I have accidently become an inspiration to many out there. This hasn't even been my intention but still I receive many emails and comments from friends and strangers telling me how my strength and determination has encouraged them to chase their own dreams and to help them achieve their goals. Thanks to my determination I can now call myself an actor, voice actor, author, singer, prop maker, event planner, presenter, promoter, Jewellery designer, world famous Harry Potter fan, a serious Harry Potter Collector, a wife and my favourite, a mum. Oh, and in 2005 I qualified as a hair dresser but because I didn't like the industry, I didn't continue with it.

One lady, Jaclyn, had been helping me in my studio for a little bit of experience in prop making. Jac was working at the Swansea Library, and in her spare time was helping a small theatre company. Jac became very good company, but to be honest I didn't know that much about her. Jac spent every Tuesday and Thursday evening with me. I didn't pay her, she just loved being there and I was so grateful for all her help. We were making the Iron Throne replica so I needed all the help I could get.

Jaclyn was very much into theatre and plays, Musicals and so on. Her passion with writing reviews, which I later found out she was exceptionally good at, so much so that she got into the final of Critic of the year in Stage magazine.

When I left the studio in Swansea, I moved into my own studio that my wonderful mum had built for me in my back garden, not long before she passed away. After this, Jaclyn and I were not able to work together again, due to her work commitments and at the time, Jac didn't have a car.

Then one random day, I received a message off her through Facebook. She told me that she really looked up to me, how I was her main inspiration and because of this, she handed in her notice at the Library, ended her tenancy at her flat and left and decided to chase her dreams and move to Scotland temporarily, to review plays for the Edinburgh Fringe Festival.

I was just so shocked, but so very proud of her. When we worked together she was quiet, but so lovely. I got the impression, that she was wasted in the Library plus the small theatre group, and I was right. Now Jaclyn is doing amazingly well and I am so proud of her. She still credits me with her success and for this I am so honoured.

Jac isn't the only person to send me messages but she most definitely was the first. I get messages or comments at least once a week. They never get boring. I love reading them. It makes me more determined to keep inspiring people. If I help just 1 more person, then it's all be worth it. Some people I get messages from are people I have known most of my life but I had no idea that I helped them. Some are total strangers, who feel that they know me even though we have never met. I don't mind this at all because it's just so nice to hear how they have turned their own lives around.

Not only do I receive messages but I also receive gifts from fans all over the world. Some of which are either hand written letters, I also recieve Harry Potter related necklaces, hand painted pictures and so many other incredible things. The other day, I was at a comic con in Newport and one of my fans came up to me and gave me a small white box. Inside was a stunning silver Deathly Hallows ring. I was so shocked. It was so lovely. I don't do these things to get gifts from people but I just receive them. I am so honoured and surprised.

When your life is a million miles an hour it's hard to keep track of who is in your life. In my eyes, if someone doesn't make you feel like yourself, brings out the worst in you or doesn't let you be the real you, you don't need them in your life. I'm thirty-six and have had my fair share of bad seeds I have had to throw away.

A relationship should be 50/50 whether that be a friendship or a romantic relationship. If it's not then don't bother. I've mentioned the meet ups I used to have with old school friends and would feel terrible afterwards, but now, I am meeting up with a group of incredible self-employed ladies who I meet for food and cocktails once a month. One massage therapist, one Psychologist and one make-up Artist. They are incredible ladies and so funny. I love them because I can be me. I go home in such a fantastic mood and feeling amazing and happy.

Nettie, Lisa, Sarah & I met in Swansea where I had my prop studio. After I left the studio, we lost contact until recently when we all decided to meet up. Well we have such a laugh and talk about anything and everything, but that's what I love. With them, what you see is what you get and it's the same with me. We all get on so well and have such a laugh. So, for that

I'm immensely grateful. We have made an agreement to meet up at least once a month to let our hair down.

Growing up you don't really pick your friends. Your parents might not like your choices but when your young you don't really care. When you get older you are more likely to choose your friends carefully. It's important and keeps you sane if you choose wisely. It's taken me a few years to realise this and with my mum no longer there for advice, it's not been easy but I'm starting to get the hang of it now.

Victoria with some of her fans in Geekedfest, Newport

**A Girl Wizard**

**An Autobiography by Victoria MacLean**

Thank you to Fahren who wanted to
create a cover for me. Thank you my lovely

# Victoria Leviosa

Victoria on the set of Ordinary Lies while filming at
The City Arms in Cardiff.

"Victoria Leviosa ha ha ha" he laughed. Tarick Cruise was laughing at his own joke but to be fair at the time, I found it quite funny. Everyone there knew what a huge Harry Potter fan I was. It was pretty much all I wore, or talked about. I was sat in the green room with my fellow SAs (aka TV extras).

I was a regular on the set of Ordinary Lies season 2 for the BBC. My role was as a regular call centre worker for a sports clothing company 'Coopers' and had been working on the production for almost four months. I have to say, it had been the best four months ever. I was working with some of the best names in the business from Con O'Neill to Angela Griffin. I was one very lucky lady. My fellow SAs and I had become like a family. We were filming in Newport and I loved it.

I would leave for work at 5.30am, head to my friend Emma's house, another SA I was working with and we would travel up together. The drive to the TV set was always a fun one if I was with Em. She was such a laugh. I get terrible travel sickness if I'm a passenger, but when I travelled with Emma, she would take my mind off it. Emma was a school teacher, but because filming for Ordinary Lies started at the beginning of the Easter holidays, she had free time to do it. We would talk about everything and anything. It was always a laugh. She was such a lovely lady too which always made my way to work a nice one. At 5.30 in the morning, the last thing I wanted was to be sat next to a negative person.

We would arrive on location half an hour early every day. Head straight up to our dressing rooms, and start to get ourselves ready. Once we were put into our costumes, we would head straight for a freshly cooked breakfast always prepared on site. After our first week, I had been nicknamed "Footwear" by Mr Con O'Neill because I had been wearing killer high heels for my costume, he was very impressed with them.

He would laugh and say, "you won't be choosing them again will you!" I laughed, because even though these shoes were almost 6 inches high, but they were the noisiest shoes on set so in the end, they were replaced with a pair of flats. This makes me laugh because in some scenes I'll be nice and tall, and in others, I'll have shrunk six inches.

The first Wednesday of week one, block one, I was sat in the green room with my fellow SAs having coffee. I suddenly heard someone mention that one of the actors was in Game of Thrones, I froze. I loved that show and was so excited to hear who it was. I was told that it was Joel Fry, who played Daenerys Targaryen's husband Hizdahr zo Loraq in season 4 and 5 and I was so excited. I was working with him oh my God! Not only Joel, but I had become friends with another Game of Thrones actor on set - Ian Davies.

He was such an amazing guy bless him. He played Morgan in season 6 of the show. Our desks were opposite each other on set so whenever the smoke machine was behind him I'd make rude comments. Ian was so tall, had blonde curly hair with the most incredible blue eyes. Bless him, he was like an over-sized teddy bear. Before you start thinking I fancied him, yes, I did and I told him this but I also told him how happy I was with my husband and he was madly in love with his fiancé.

I believe that if someone is attractive, life is too short to keep that to yourself. In fact, the first words I ever spoke to him were "Your eyes are gorgeous!"

Being on set was one of the best jobs in the world, but because of the distance, I barely broke even financially. We got paid just under £100 a day for a twelve-hour shoot. Take away the agencies cut and I think I was taking home £81. That £81 had to cover my fuel which was a two-hour drive back and forth to set, child care, my clothes, and anything else I needed to get for that day.

For Ordinary Lies we had to provide our own clothes. Some of you will be asking, why would you do it for no money? Well the truth is, I loved it. They say, find a job you love and you'll never work a day again in your life. Well this is the job I love. Yes, the money is shit, but I don't care. Last week I was working with Jack Whitehall and Steve Spiers, so I'm not going to complain. I have met and worked with some incredible actors from Harry Potter, Game of Thrones and Dr Who. Plus, some of which have now become friends of mine.

I am very much liked and loved on set. I feel this is because, I'm a happy go lucky person. I enjoy what I do, I don't go all 'Fan Girl' on them and I do as I'm told. I am always early to set and am very dedicated to the job at hand. I believe you should treat people how you want to be treated. If they don't treat you the same way, then you don't need to even waste your breath on them but don't be rude, don't react and just step aside. These sorts of people will never change, so there is no need to try, they most certainly don't have a place in my life, but if I'm working with them, I'm just very professional and I get the job done. Once the shoot was finished, I'd get back into my car and make my way home to my family.

If I was to choose my favourite actor I have worked with, I'd say it would have to be Ian Davies. Mostly because he was just so nice and friendly. The most incredible actor I know has got to be my acting couch, Ross O'Hennessy who played the Lord of Bones in season five of Game of Thrones. I just love Ross and his fiancé Emma is just so incredibly lovely. I haven't known Ross for long, but we were put in contact with each other a few months ago when he asked me to help him out with my Iron Throne for a charity event to raise money to help save Blackwood Little Theatre. I was told he did acting classes in

Cardiff so I had to take part. I've only been doing them for four weeks but I just love them.

We regularly visit Comic Cons with the Iron Throne now. When we attend, we get VIP treatment too. It's amazing. Plus, because we get VIP treatment, we get to have lunch with so many celebrities. I remember just visiting Wales Comic Con in Wrexham earlier this year. I was sat with my friend Jaclyn, and started having a chat with a guy about other conventions. Turns out this guy was none other than Chris Rankin (aka Percy Weasley from Harry Potter). The same day, I shook hands with Jason Momoa (aka Khal Drogo from Game of Thrones). My God he was just gorgeous and I couldn't help but stare!

I want to be an actor, so much. Not to be famous because I feel I'm already on my way there with everything else. It's because I truly love it. I want to find out what I'm capable of. What I can do with my craft. I just wish I could explore it more. They say you need to be hungry for it well I bloody am. I love it. I love it and for that short time, becoming that person that character. I want it more than anything, well not more than Harry Potter but it's a close second. Adam is the first person to believe in me. To feel that this could be my true path. Since November last year I have been saying to him, something big is coming and when it comes to money, we are going to be fine. It's to do with me but I just don't know what.

This is nothing new for me. Just the other day I thought to myself I need to get buildings insurance on our house just in case someone drives through our wall, then only a few days later, someone drove through Adams parents wall just up the road from us. Spooky. Today I could have sworn that Adam was shouting at someone for hitting our car, but he hadn't so I'm just wait in a few days for someone to hit our car. Just a few days later, someone hit our car when it was parked at the van hire company. Made a lovely meant in the side of the car, but because of where it was parked, there was nothing we could do.

I can feel when my daughter is scared. I know when things aren't right. It hardly happens but when it doesn't I'm very rarely wrong. Ok yes, you can doubt me but have you ever suddenly started singing a song in your head and when you have gone to turn on the radio it's playing the same song? Or gone to phone or text a friend and they are trying to contact you? Lately I had the feeling of I must text Jac, she would then reply that she was amazed that I always knew when she was feeling low and to text her. Crazy stuff!

Though they say what makes a good actor, is someone who has been through so much in their life. I think I kind of qualify for that. There isn't much I haven't been through but it's all a learning curve. If I was told I could go back and change something in my past, other than keeping my mum on the phone for longer, I don't think I would change anything. It's made me who I am today. My mum never said no to me, she always told me to learn from my mistakes. I'm very proud to say I think it's worked. Besides how many teenagers listen when their parents when they are told NO anyway.

I'm looking forward to going further with my acting. I love it. The rush is amazing. Learning your lines is brilliant and makes you feel so alive. It's a bloody long and boring process mind. It can be hours and hours of sitting around on set waiting for a different camera position or actors being blocked or some technical difficulties but the trick is to take what makes you comfortable with you. Lots of films on your phone or laptop, comfy slippers, an enjoyable book, and a really good phone charger lol. It's all important. I never travel light but I like to go prepared for anything.

The truth is, I don't know what's around the corner. Whatever is waiting for me though, I will face it head on. It's my life and my God I'm going to live it!

Victoria talking live on Bay TV, Swansea

Victoria on set with BBC presenter

Andrew Marr with her Iron Throne

# Nineteen Years Later

Victoria during a photo shoot with part of her
Harry Potter and Fantastic Beasts collection.

Where I have got today is amazing. I get boxes of Harry Potter
and Fantastic Beasts memorabilia sent to me for free just so I
can advertise them. The number one company I go to for all my
Noble Collection items is Moving Pictures Exeter. Collin and
Sam have become good friends and yes, we were friends before
they started sending me free items. They are an incredible
couple and I truly admire their generosity. Thank you both. I
love you. I have fans all over the world because apparently, I'm

a really lovely person and inspire people to fight for what they want and believe in. I didn't aim for this, it's just happened.

I get calls from TV companies and Radio stations all the time because of my unofficial connection with Harry Potter. I also get contacted by companies not attached to the Wizarding World like Britain's Got Talent. It's a long story but one I will enjoy telling another time. I get invited to exclusive events by such incredible people as MinaLima. When I met Miraphora Mina I was in shock when she knew who I was. It was so lovely. I introduced myself "hi my lovely. I'm Victoria" and she said, "I know." Best evening of my life. I just beamed at her. She was such an incredibly kind and incredibly creative lady who, alongside Eduardo Lima had just finished working on Fantastic Beasts and Where to Find Them which was released on the 18th of November this year. The art work is out of this world. I was never a history fan, but thanks to the work they had put in to Fantastic Beasts, I was hooked. I even started looking for old style New Your memorabilia such as, city maps, binoculars, and more. I even managed to get an old fashioned dress marker that was designed in the 1920s. The city map I bought is dated 1926. Such a good find and an incredible piece of history.

I was asked to meet MinaLima in London after I emailed them about doing promo work for them. Being asked to meet them was such a huge deal because I'm such a massive fan of their work. I didn't know them but their work spoke volumes to me. Their enthusiasm and passion for their art and then love for what they do just screams at you from each and every piece of art they create. When I met Eduardo Lima he was not what I expected at all. He was just so very lovely, and such a pleasure to talk to. If I could and they EVER had time, I'd love to just have a sit down with them both and talk creating. I wear my heart on my sleeve so it would be a brilliant conversation indeed. Bless Eduardo, when I met him, he gave me gifts. I didn't expect anything, I was just so grateful to chat with him. In fact, I was so inspired after meeting Eduardo and seeing their work in person from the Harry Potter films that I re decorated my entire bathroom in MinaLima, Harry Potter Weasley Wizard Wheezes style.

I'm an extremely humble person and as I have mentioned before, I am my own worst critic. I'm writing this book as someone who is desperate to tell her story. Hoping I can help others, but I still think about my life and wander how I have become so lucky with everything I have. With everyone in my life and my incredible family who I would die for. Im not brilliant with compliments. Don't get me wrong, I love reading them but then I struggle to reply. I don't want to sound big headed so most of the time my reply is "awwwwwwwww Thank you so much" because I just don't know what to say. Some people send me horrible messages, but now after realising no matter who I am, I cant change how they feel so I just ignore them, or my fans step in and take it on them selves. I don't encourage this, but its nice to finally see people want to stick up for me as I have never had this before. Over the last 6 months I have been stalked by 2 people and the police have been involved, but I know I'm ok. I'm safe, they don't know where I live and these 2 people are utter cowards. They just do what many jealous and sad individuals do, hide behind their keyboards. However, I simply wish them love, luck and happiness in their lives and move on.

On the bright side, I get gifts sent to me through the post from fans as far as Australia all because of what I have done. It's not been encouraged, because I feel hugely grateful being given something simple like a free Harry Potter bookmark. That to me is so amazing and things like hand written notes, but I've had really expensive Noble Collection items too. My most favourite part is getting to meet Harry Potter fans from all over the UK when I visit Comic Cons as a guest or through my

Harry Potter UK and Fantastic Beasts UK Facebook pages. I love to chat with them. They are always so enthusiastic and loveable. I could never get bored.

In the last year, I have met 6 incredible people. Kelly White, Sean Valentine, Beverley Jenkinson, Janice Burnett, Charlotte Jukes and Johnny Blue. These incredible friends work at the Harry Potter studios in London and Johnnie I have known through collecting Harry Potter. I have to say, they have become really good friends of mine.

Sean Valentine runs Valentines Miniatures. He is an incredible talent. Sean, not only is an incredibly talented hair dresser but as a hobby, he makes incredibly detailed and intricate dolls houses and music box rooms. Earlier this year, I was tagged in a post on Facebook by my friend Janice. The post was about a Harry Potter music box room that Valentines Miniatures was making of the Hogwarts Gryffindor common room. My God it was incredible. I was in love. I contacted the company and over time Sean and I became good friends. He's such an incredible man who is one of the nicest and most caring people you could ever meet. He's so talented that Harrods in London, offered him a job in their doll house department of their store but because Sean didn't want to leave Swansea or move to London, he gratefully declined. I really do love Sean and have badgered him to sell me his next Harry Potter, Hogwarts creation.

Kelly, Monica and I are going to meet Warwick Davies in the studios soon. Warwick played numerous Harry Potter characters is someone I have met before but not for years and I wasn't collecting Harry Potter autographs back then. I can't wait because I just love spending time with Kelly. My friends mean the world to me.

Johnnie is from Scotland. He has met JK Rowling on a few occasions and has done incredible events to raise money for JK Rowling's charity Limos. He is such an incredible friend who I value dearly. When Adam and I first visited Edinburgh back in March, Johnnie he took us to the Balmoral suit where JK Rowling was filmed finishing Harry Potter book 'Harry Potter and the Deathly Hallows' what an incredible day that was and one I will never forget. Thank you my lovely, you're a friend for life.

As for my incredible page editors, Beverley, Janice amd now Charlotte, well I honestly couldn't of asked for more. They have bought some incredible new highlights to my social media and to fans all over the world. They are all so much fun and love what they do. I feel very blessed to have them on my page and in my life. Thank you girls xx

My pages Harry Potter UK, HarryPotterUK on Instagram and Twitter and my Harry Potter UK YouTube channel have all helped me to stay connected with my fans and to many more Harry Potter superfans out there just like me.

I have fans on my Victoria Maclean Facebook page too who purely follow me as fans of well, me. It's amazing how many people you can reach these days just through social media. I wish I could meet all of you in person but it's simply not possible, and thanks to my friend Charlotte LR Kane, I now have a website too. VictoriaMaclean.co.uk.

The truth is, I'm just like them. I'm obsessed and love everything about Harry Potter. I live, eat and breath it. Every day. No breaks. My house is over flowing but it is me. It's my life. It's who I am. I will never change. I've gone from being someone who was digging a deep dark hole for herself to someone who is standing tall showing the world who she has become. With an incredible husband and the most amazing children who I would give it all up in a heartbeat for. My family are everything to me and there aren't many of us left.

People won't understand this but very deep down I will always love my dad but he is now out of my life for good and it will stay this way. I don't want anything to do with him anymore. He was brilliant with my daughter when she was little. I think he saw her as another chance and treated her like a princess. Like he would treat other children. Like I wanted my dad to of treated me when I was living at home but I just wish he had said he was sorry or tried to stay in contact with me, or my children more but he didn't. I now know the truth about what my dad did to us and it sickens me to my stomach. Dad, mum always told me if I needed to talk to you and you wouldn't listen to write you a letter, so in a way this is me doing that. I now know the truth and you know what that means. You will always be my dad but I'm sorry it's too late now. I don't love you like I used to anymore and I hope I never see you again. You can't change the past and you never tried to amend it either!

To those of you who bullied me. You know who you are. Some of you have become friends but I will never fully trust you. I don't trust many people at all to be honest. Look at how far I have come even after what you did for fun. Think about that for a moment. To those of you who still bully, look at how long this has stayed with me and affected me all these years. Do you really want to do that to someone else? I'm a much stronger person than most. If you had bullied anyone who wasn't as strong, they may have end up taking their own life. Think about that. Think about the effect you are having on those people suffering in silence. You need to stop. One day you could go too far!

Make the most of your family because that phone call or face to face you have with them, may be the last you will ever have. Cherish your family with every bone in your body, with every breath you take. I will never see my mum again but you could still see yours. You only have one. The problem I have is my mum never got to see my success. She died before I became famous and had fans meeting me and asking for my autograph. She never got to see me on telly or hear me on the radio or see me in magazines but I know she is watching me from up there. In her own Wizarding World.

I realised that all you need to do when you want to get somewhere in life is focus. No matter where you have come from or how you started. If you want it that much, you will get it. I have pushed and pushed myself every day. I work bloody hard. I am always updating myself and my work. Looking for new angles. It's never too late to figure out what you want to become in life.

Harry Potter has brought me that. JK Rowling fought for her dream just because all she wanted to be was a writer. Becoming rich and famous was just a bonus. I will fight for what I want. No one is in my way but me. I want to be so many things so am fighting for it all to see what happens. My way is to take 1 day at a time. 1 step at a time. Your path has already been laid out before you, all you have to do is follow it. What have you got to lose?

I want to be an actor so I am exploring it. The second I start to doubt myself, I may as well quit. I can do it I just have to fight. I want to be known as a world-famous Harry Potter fan, well I have got that one already but it doesn't stop me from not pushing even more.

With me what you see is what you get. Yes, I am really that nice. yes, I am really that laid back and no I couldn't care less what country you're from, what colour or race you are, or your religion. I treat people how I want to be treated. Everyone is human. We are all the same. We were born the same way and we will die the same way. I have fans from all walks of life and some of the poorest of countries but that's what I love about Harry Potter. It's universal. It's one big happy family and I love you all.

Writing this autobiography started off being easy. The further I got, the harder it was to write my memories down but I've finished. It's been like a form of therapy to be honest. I'd like to say I've enjoyed it. Well I have sort of. The beginning was hard but towards the end when I think of how far I have come, the hurdles I have overcome. My children. My family and my friends. I'm the luckiest person I know and to think, my ways and my actions have inspired so very many people all over the world to help themselves and to chase their dreams. It just amazes me but to think I've gone from a girl who lived in fear to a lady who has everything.

Not to mention an obsessed Harry Potter fan who won't leave the house without adorning something Harry Potter related, I have a lot to thank JK Rowling for. She has saved me from so much. Not to mention helped me learn to read and write and to take the plunge to write my very first novel. Harry Potter is my life. It is part of me now. It runs through my veins. I'm eternally grateful for the boy wizard and 19 years later, when people ask me.....

"After all this time?"

I will reply with....


"Always"



To be continued........

37249168R00102

Printed in Great Britain
by Amazon